The Devotional Life of a Pastor's Wife

By Various Authors

Exterior cover design by Natalie Decosta

Printed material by Frame vector created by BiZkettE1 Freepik.com - This cover has been designed using resources from Freepik.com

Interior page design by Natalie Decosta & Sophie Holt

This book is a work compiled by twenty-one authors. Each Testimony and story are true. To maintain anonymity some minor details have been edited.

The Devotional Life of a Pastor's Wife/ Project lead by Charlotte Claxton; Foreword by Anonymous

Other authors include Chantella Claxton, Sophie Holt, Hannah Sekimpi, Hannah Crisp, Natalie Decosta, Joanne Dale, Penny Boddy, Emma Ruzvidzo, Coral Perry, Becky Remigio, Lisa Claxton, Sarah Jenkins, Kadi Ikutiyinu, Vicky Brick, Mariah Brick, Hollie Galt, Trudy Bennett, Jackie Wilkie, Natasha Nichols, Pam Kyriacou.

ISBN: 9798562721303

THIS BOOK BELONGS TO

....

....

<u>For every woman who was, is or desires to be the wife of a pastor</u>

Our prayer is that this book will further equip you as a Christian and cause you to fall in love with Jesus more and more.

ACKNOWLEDGEMENTS

'The Team' aka 'The Armour Bearers'

Each of the following women were a part of the 'original' WhatsApp group that inspired this book, without them this book would not have been possible. Every task that has been delegated to them has been fully embraced and efficiently completed, they have never let me down. Every devotion they have contributed has and will cause the reader to feel encouraged, challenged and inspired. Together we have fasted and prayed that this book would bless and revolutionise the life of a pastor's wife.

Chantella Claxton- Thank you for your consistency, words of encouragement and fantastic administrative skills.

Hannah Sekimpi: Thank you for your unwavering support, your time in formatting the manuscript and for your care of other PW's.

Hannah Crisp: Thank you for being a listening ear and for making me laugh.

Natalie Decosta: Thank you for your tireless efforts on the design of the book; your skills have been paramount in this project. You are the reason it looks so beautiful. Thank you.

Sophie Holt: Thank you for the gorgeous artwork you contributed to the internal pages of the book. Thank you for picking up the phone (mostly late at night) when I couldn't contain my excitement about a new idea, devotion or when I had a question.

I thank everyone one of you for your friendship.

Other Pastors, Evangelists and Missionary Wives

Joanne Dale – Penny Boddy – Emma Ruzvidzo – Coral Perry – Becky Remigio – Lisa Claxton – Sarah Jenkins – Kadi Ikutiyinu– Vicky Brick – Mariah Brick – Hollie Galt – Trudy Bennett – Jacqui Wilkie – Natasha Nichols – Pam Kyriacou

For your contributions, they are what brings the depth and flavour to this book. Thank You.

Doctrinal proof-readers

Pastor Daniel Crisp – Pastor Sam Holt – Pastor Adam Claxton –

Pastor Lewis Claxton

These men willingly took on the important challenge of checking every devotion and testimony to make sure that every scripture fitted the thought. A time-consuming task on top of all that is required of them nevertheless they did it. Thank you.

Editors

Trisha Malone

A wonderful, faithful woman who desired to glorify God by willingly taking on the mammoth task of editing the 261 devotions and 52 testimonies. Although she had never edited before the team and I believed she possessed the skills to do it. We approached her and she at that point (during Covid19) had been praying for the Lord to open a door for her to do something for Him; This was her answered prayer, God is good. She has been efficient and hard working. Thank you.

David Drum

David has been instrumental in the completion of this project; his editing skills have added the sleek touch to each devotion and testimony. We are so grateful for your lastminute.com interventions, they are remarkable. Thank you.

Proof-readers

Delphine Mensah & Cheryl Nembhard

Thank you for diligent efforts in putting this book through the refining process. You've done a beautiful job.

Other

On behalf of myself and the team, we want to thank **Our families**.

Thank you for your love and prayers. There have been many periods during this amazing project when our minds and time have been consumed however you have been patient and released us, we thank God for you and love you until the ends of the earth.

Pastor Paul Boddy

For your support during this book and thank you for believing in us to do it.

INTRODUCTION

Hello, my name is Charlotte Claxton. I am a Christian, a mother, and a Pastor's wife.

Who knew that 2020 would be a year that could change life as we know it, potentially for ever! I want to tell you a little about how the Coronavirus pandemic has changed my life and the lives of other pastor's wives around me, thus inspiring this book.

The rumours that the UK was going into lockdown were spreading around mid-February. If I'm honest (although I wished the circumstances weren't so horrific) I couldn't wait, I love being with my family. As I began to prepare for lockdown, stockpiling toilet paper (just kidding), school supplies, and food, I pondered how this pandemic would affect our church. I considered the different circumstances the people in our congregation were living and dealing with (some with mental health issues, underlying health conditions, nurses, doctors, elderly, single mums, new converts) and wondered how was this going to affect them. *How was I going to engage with the ladies for potentially months? More importantly, how could I help them maintain a spiritual mindset and encourage them to stay focused on the Word and prayer?* The love I have for these ladies drove me to prayer, 'Lord you have to show me what to do.'

The Holy Spirit inspired me to invite the ladies to participate in posting a devotion on our WhatsApp group. I challenged them to use a scripture from their daily bible reading, write a thought to accompany it, and a prayer at the end if they felt necessary. It was a worthy shot in the dark if it meant we could all stay connected with each other and to Jesus. To my amazement, sixteen women responded. Words cannot express how insightful, encouraging, and motivating it was to read their devotions every morning during a pandemic; God used every one of them.

My mind also turned to pioneer churches, mainly Pastor's wives. A church that is not yet established with core families and individuals could be detrimentally affected in a time like this. 'Goodness,' I thought, 'they're going to need a lot of encouragement, why not do the same with them but on a different forum?'

I invited five friends and all responded, a great result! Two and a half months into writing devotions the Holy Spirit challenged me to produce a book using the devotionals we had already written as the base of it.

How does the book work?

Instead of producing one massive book that has over 400 pages, we wanted to create something a little more manageable and less costly to purchase. We have therefore created four books that contain three months' worth of material, one for every season.

Days one through five consist of **Devotionals**.

The sixth day is an empty double page spread entitled '**Study/ Sermon notes**' to encourage you to write your own devotion, study a scripture you have read in the week, take notes on a sermon, or journal about what God is speaking to you.

The seventh day is a **Testimony** day, an account written by a Pastor's wife about her salvation or experience on the harvest field.

Bible in a year/Bible in two years

This book includes a custom made 'Bible in a year' and 'Bible in two-year' program, that is at the bottom of every page like this:

Y1 - Genesis 1 & 2 / Y2 - Matthew 2 & 3

('Y1' refers to the first year where you will be reading through approximately half of the bible. 'Y2' refers to the second year where you will complete it by reading the other half of the bible. Alternatively, you can read '**Y1 & Y2**' at the same time and complete the bible in only one year.)

The struggle to maintain bible reading has become increasingly more apparent. Sometimes you must go back to basics; picking up your bible on the odd occasion will not carry you through. Therefore, we have produced a simple plan that accommodates all lifestyles, a plan that can get you consistently reading God's Word (without being overwhelmed). A plan that requires discipline yet inspires achievement. The plan works through one book of the bible at a time, alternating between the Old and New Testaments.

Additionally, in the back of the first book you will find a list of (whittled down) **recommended reading** that covers a range of topics which have helped many Pastor's wives over the years. We hope this helps you!

Who are the authors?

The authors (in all four volumes) consist of thirty-three wives of current pastors, evangelists, and missionaries, as well as those who have served in this capacity in the past. This mix was thought important to get both a current dimension and to glean from the women who have returned home after their time on the harvest field as their wisdom and knowledge bring a special aspect of insight and depth to the book.

The nature of the book

I'm sure you have already gathered that we are not professional writers, but we are women with experience, spiritual revelation, and a desire to serve. In my initial pitch to invite these women to join the project, I understood that some would find it a breeze, some a challenge, and others an impossible task. I stressed that their writing ability meant nothing (that's why we have editors), it was in fact their insight and experience we desired.

Included in this book are devotionals and testimonies that are raw, insightful, unusual, deep, heart-breaking, witty, inspiring, uplifting, encouraging, and convicting, but I can assure you, all will leave you with hope and vision.

The purpose of this book

There are a handful of books written for the Pastor's wife out there, but it seems, nothing quite like this. Over the years, having spoken to many Pastor's wives, I have developed a growing concern regarding their personal relationship with God. You will invest in what you love.

Luke 10:27 (NIV)
He answered, 'Love the LORD your God with all your heart and with all your soul and with all your strength and with all your mind...'

For some Pastor's wives it seems that their primary investments are elsewhere. Children, possessions, and even the ministry can consume you to the point that you lose a sense of urgency when it comes to having an intimate, active, and a blossoming relationship with your Saviour. My prayer is that every Pastor's wife, strong in the Lord or not, will dedicate themselves to seeking Him with all their soul, strength, and mind. With this in place I can almost guarantee that the best of life is yet to come.

Here are a few objectives for the Pastor's wife using this book:

- Cause her to prioritise a devotional life of prayer, reading, and studying the word of God; and as a result, change, grow, be restored, have fruit, and be equipped for the good fight.
- Help her to understand and embrace the importance of her example.
- Inspiration for the harvest field.
- Clarity to this role she has been called to.
- Bring unity; we are all in this together.

'It's not always easy, but it's simple.'

This has become my motto in living my Christian life. I speak from experience when I say that I spent years trying to fight the 'duvet demon' to get up and pray in the morning. What I found is that fighting the flesh is not without effort, but it is a straightforward task. Fighting for the routine of praying and reading in the morning, coupled with studying the word at a point during the week, has brought huge change in my life, and I pray it will for you also.

Why Pastor's wives?

Maintaining a consistent, close connection with God is a challenge for almost every Christian. It seems that once a couple of steps have been taken into the ministry, the devotional life can be one of the first things to be assaulted. The pressures build up, duties pile up, exhaustion sets in, and before you know it, instead of feeling victorious you are left thirsty and dried out. I want to declare to you that this does not have to be the norm.

The Pastor's wife is the silent server. Like a backbone, her ability to function practically and spiritually affects her husband, children, church, the community around her, and potentially the world. My prayer is that she can operate consistently whilst soaking in the joys of life and the wonderous blessing of the cross.

The proceeds of the book

100% of the profit will be donated to world evangelism.

Charlotte Claxton x

FOREWORD

At the beginning of the COVID-19 lockdown, I was asked to be involved in a new lockdown challenge: produce a devotion inspired by daily reading and post it on the WhatsApp group on my allocated day. The purpose was to help each of us dig deeper into the word of God, develop a stronger prayer life, and maintain relationships during that difficult period. My initial reaction was, 'Me? Really? Gosh, I don't know if I'm able!' I felt inadequate, but nevertheless I enjoyed the challenge, so I agreed to participate.

If I can be transparently and painfully honest before lockdown my mind was in shatters and so was my relationship with God. I had fallen into a deep pit. I was questioning my worth, wrestling with condemnation, and feeling entirely useless. I had self-hatred and thoughts of punishing myself, for being undeserving of everything I had started to creep in. It got to the point where I didn't feel worthy to hold my child. I felt disbelief in my husband's words of love for me as I could no longer love myself. I felt so alone. The shame of these thoughts were unbearable, knowing they were ungodly, and continually saying to myself, 'Pastor's wives shouldn't think like this.' I felt like I was sinking and there was nothing I could do about it.

Little did I know, God was fighting for me and He was making a way out. The challenge of writing a devotion every week caused me to read the bible like never before. I experienced how relatable, encouraging, and challenging it was, and the more I read and prayed, the more I knew God and hungered for Him. Right there was the beginning of my deliverance.

When I look back, it's bizarre to think that I genuinely couldn't work out the solution because I *always* fully believed that Jesus was *always* the answer. Since this change in my devotional life, I can see clearly again. It is becoming easier to rationalise and look forward. I am slowly but surely growing in wisdom and discernment, and instead of falling apart at the first hurdle I am taking a step back and assessing the situation and thus bringing it before God. I've learnt that God's timing is perfect down to the very second. He peels back layers bit by bit and gives you the resources to deal with all aspects of life. He is all we need and all we can depend on.

But the very hairs of your head are all numbered. Do not fear; therefore, you are of more value than many sparrows (Matthew 10:30-32 NKJV). I received this verse from a preacher within the first few months of my salvation. Now, possibly for the first time, I believed it. Why? Because I have started to know God for myself on a personal level.

This book is a tool to help you develop or renew your own devotional life and draw you into a deeper relationship with Him. There is a direct correlation between seeking God and deliverance. The joy I feel now is no coincidence. I have yet to master the discipline of a consistent devotional life, but now I have the revelation I need to keep fighting for it because of the dimension that has been added to my life by viewing God as a personal God, a literal father, and a sincere friend.

Anon

January 1st – *Greatest Asset*

Y1 - GEN 1 & 2 / Y2 – 1 THESS 1 & 2

Proverbs 18:22 (NKJV)
He who finds a wife finds a good thing and obtains favour from the lord.

Every one of us has gone into a partnership with the man of our choice… hopefully. Being a pastor's wife was perhaps never on your radar, especially if you married before becoming a Christian, but you did make the promise, 'better or worse, richer or poorer, sickness and health,' all descriptive of your role as a minister's wife. God says about marriage in Ephesians 5:31 that, '… the two shall become one,' which simply means that you are part of the package! God calls couples into the ministry.

What does that role mean to you? Have you thought about how you wish to conduct yourself in this position? Do you understand how important and essential you are?

Having spoken to many pastor's wives over the years, it has come to my attention that the majority willingly supported their husbands in entering the ministry but had absolutely no clue what their role was in accompanying him. You may possess the ability to sing, teach women, write a Christmas play, or handle a Sunday school class of boisterous children. Or, alternatively, the notion of any of these may leave you feeling completely intimidated and unqualified. Many of us wouldn't, initially, have considered ourselves to be 'pastor's wife' material because we thought it required being the spiritual version of Wonder Woman.

The truth is that we are free to choose how we express ourselves. We come in different shapes, sizes, ages, races, and personalities. It's not your gifting that makes you an asset to the ministry, it's you. You are the gift! Your husband's greatest asset in the ministry is a wife who loves him; a wife who knows how to pray and study the Word of God; a wife who is independent in her faith, has developed her own convictions, and conducts herself in righteousness with a heart that glorifies God. God has called you to be a wife that although has a fallen nature, seeks to be the best Christian she can. This scripture indicates that your husband finds favour because of you!

Rest assured that you are not a spare part, you are vital. His greatest asset!

January 2nd – *Overwhelming Grace*
Y1 - GEN 3 & 4 / Y2 - 1 THESS 3 & 4

John 1:16 (AMP)
"For out of His fullness [the superabundance of His grace and truth] we have all received grace upon grace [spiritual blessing upon spiritual blessing, favour upon favour, and gift heaped upon gift]."

God shows grace to all who make mistakes, fall into temptation, or even backslide, when we should be expecting the opposite. Grace is given rather than what we deserve (Thank God); it is an unmerited favour from God. What a miracle that He has saved, delivered, and restored us by His grace. This verse gives the picture that He has so much grace it is spilling over. I'm reminded of lyrics from a song by David Crowder, "If His grace is an ocean, we're all sinking... I don't have time to maintain these regrets when I think about how He loves us."

There can be times in our lives when we take God's grace for granted, but if we truly think about who we are and where we came from it can become a fresh revelation. He will use events in life to remind us and highlight His grace. We experienced God's grace at salvation, but His abundant grace strengthens and sustains us as we live for Him. By our own strength we will fail, but His grace is sufficient and new each day. Through His grace we can be equipped to face our daily struggles and trials.

2 Corinthians 12:9 (NKJV)
"And He said to me, "My grace is sufficient for you, for My strength is made perfect in weakness." Therefore, most gladly I will rather boast in my infirmities, that the power of Christ may rest upon me."

His grace is overwhelmingly amazing to think of. Take time today to ponder His grace in your life.

Lord, I thank you for your abundant grace, that you have saved and restored me, when I deserve nothing at all. Help me to remain grateful and not take for granted what you have done for me. Let your grace strengthen me each day, through trials and difficulties. Amen.

January 3rd – *Study Scripture*
Y1 - GEN 5 & 6 / Y2 - 1 THESS 5

2 Tim 3:16-17 (NKJV)
All scripture is given by inspiration of God, and is profitable for doctrine, for reproof, for correction, for instruction in righteousness, that the man of God may be complete, thoroughly equipped for every good work.

(MSG transliteration)
Every part of scripture is God-breathed and useful in one way or another - showing us truth, exposing our rebellion, correcting our mistakes, training us to live in God's way. Through the word we are put together and shaped for the task God has for us.

This verse tells us that it is the Word of God that brings change, encouragement, inspiration, faith, direction, wisdom, correction, and advice. We could search the world twice-over and find no other source that compares; *but are you really convinced of that?* Paul said, 'faith *comes* by hearing, and hearing by the word of God (Romans 10:17).'

Are you in love with the Word of God? Do you really believe that it is God's Word that is the foundation of our faith?

What would happen if you began to bathe your life in His Word? If you meditated on His Word daily could it change your outlook? Would miracles happen if you started to speak out God's Word to your children (no matter how young), friends, parents, and people on the street? If you stood in faith on His Word would you see an empowering effect when trying times come? Yes! Start today by memorizing and internalizing a verse. Write it on sticky notes and post around your house (read Deuteronomy 6:4-9). And don't forget to plan a time tomorrow to do the same.

Lord Jesus, please give me a burning desire to love your Word. I know it is profitable for many things, and I want more of You in my life. Thank You for your Word! Help me to depend on it more and more, and as a result, people would see more of You in me. Amen

January 4th – *Persistent Prayer*

Y1 - GEN 7 & 8 / Y2 - 2 CHRON 1 & 2

Mathew 15:28 (NKJV)
Then Jesus answered and said to her, 'O woman, great is your faith! Let it be to you as you desire.' And her daughter was healed from that very hour.

When we read this verse, we feel like this woman received an immediate answer to her prayer and we want the same in our circumstance. However, if you read the whole story, the evidence of her faith and the reason Jesus called it 'great' was her persistence. A few things stand out from this story:

1. Jesus at first seems to ignore her, but she persists to the point the disciples urge Him to tell her to go away because she was 'bothering' them with her begging (vs. 23). She is not put off but keeps asking (persistence).
2. Then Jesus tells her 'no' because she is a Gentile, and He was sent to 'the people of Israel.' She persists in asking (vs. 24-25).
3. Then Jesus says earlier (vs. 26) that one of the most offensive things we ever read coming out of His mouth, 'It isn't right to take food from the children and throw it to the dogs'. This woman's faith is being tested, but she doesn't give up or get mad. She continues to ask, 'even dogs are allowed to eat the scraps (vs. 27).'
4. Then Jesus responds, 'great is your faith' because of her persistence and heals her daughter.

Many would have given up after the first request, but this woman was desperate. We can only imagine that she had tried everything else and yet the daughter she loved was no better. She heard about Jesus working miracles and she knew it was her only hope. She could not stop asking until she got an answer. There is a need for persistent prayer in our lives as well. Don't give up before your answer comes. Don't allow discouragement, distraction, or neglect to keep you from the miracles you need. Renew your commitment today to consistent, persistent, and insistent prayer.

Colossians 4:2 (TEV)
Be persistent in prayer, and keep alert as you pray, always giving thanks to God.

January 5th – *Tone Deaf*
Y1 - GEN 9 & 10 / Y2 - 2 CHRON 3 & 4

Matthew 9:30 (NIV)
And their sight was restored. Jesus warned them sternly, "See that no one knows about this." But they went out and spread the news about him all over that region.

You've heard the saying, 'It's not what you say, it's how you say it.' The tone we use often implies something we did not intend with our words. It's easy to let our mood shine through so that our words become sharp like knives. And, since it has been said that women speak far more words per day than men, that gives us far more reason to be mindful of our tone of voice.

In our text Jesus uses His tone to express the importance of His command. This is a great example of a man having authority in his speech. The text doesn't say, 'Then wagging His finger, Jesus addressed His disciples with a high-pitched scream.' Of course not! Jesus always conducted himself with decorum. If we give into the guaranteed opportunities to 'fly off the handle' it will achieve nothing and exhibits our lack of self-control and discredits our character.

Proverbs 15:1 (Mess)
A gentle response defuses anger, but a sharp tongue kindles a temper-fire.

The tone we use can defuse anger or kindle a temper-fire. *Have you ever heard someone speak with an attitude or tone that is displeasing (normally someone close to you) only to realise that they have learnt it from you?* We owe it to the people we interact with to be mindful of our tone when in conversation. Let's take a leaf out of Jesus's book and start thinking about how we use our voice to convey what we mean and in doing so earn the respect of the people around us.

Thank you, Jesus, for your example. I acknowledge that my tone of voice is not always appreciated and can bring division at times. I ask you to forgive me for the disrespect I caused people through it. Help me to be aware of this issue going forward and bring conviction when I need it. In Jesus name, Amen.

January 6th – *Testimony*

Joanne's Salvation Story

I was raised on a council estate in one of the most deprived areas of the UK where high unemployment, teenage pregnancy, crime, and domestic violence were commonplace. With no father or father figure in my life, my Mum worked her fingers to the bone to provide for us four children. Mum relocated the family when I was 9 to make a better life for us; however, it didn't work out and we ended up in a horrendous cycle of homelessness, with violence being part of Mum's relationships. It was so disruptive. With no friends and no schooling, I became withdrawn and insecure. Social services threatened to take me and my brother into care and it was at this time that Mum became desperate, exhausted from doing absolutely all she could. She cried out to God, and after being told there was no way we were going to be housed, the council called her the next day and gave us emergency housing. This was the first miracle I experienced.

Finally, I began to feel like I had some security, but when my brother started getting into trouble and our home was raided by police, this was ripped from my life again. I began to self-harm to vent my anger and frustration. I vowed I would never have that council estate life or problematic relationships, poverty, and brokenness like my Mum. However, my first relationship at the age of 14 began to reflect this same cycle! I ended up with a man who was possessive, controlling, and abusive. After 3 years I knew I had to get out of that relationship and my life had to change, but I didn't know how. One night I was walking our dog and I just kept thinking, 'I don't want this life.' Suddenly, the phrase popped into my head, 'There are two ways out: you can either kill yourself, or you can serve God.' I had no idea what serving God meant, but I knew I didn't want to die, nor did I want the life I had. So, I thought I would find a church for that Sunday.

When I arrived home, there was a leaflet from a church for a concert for the very next night – I knew I had to go! I went to the concert and could see that there was something different about these people; they were so happy and obviously had something that I did not. I remember thinking to myself, 'I want what they have!' At the end of the concert I responded to the invitation: I prayed and asked Jesus to forgive me of my sins and to come into my life. I began to weep and felt a huge weight lift from my shoulders as God's love filled my soul. I walked home feeling like I was walking on air, excited, but not quite understanding what had happened. Through God's help I managed to get the courage to end the relationship with my boyfriend. Jesus began to bring complete healing in my life from the hurt and abuse. I now look back and cannot believe that hurt, insecure girl was me. I have now been a Christian for over 25 years and Jesus has blessed my life so much: Even though I came from a broken home, God has blessed me with a wonderful and loving husband; even though I was brought up without a father, God has blessed me with beautiful children who have a secure and happy home.

January 7th - *Study & Sermon notes*

Y1 - PS 2 / Y2 - PS 106

January 8th – *My Creator*

Y1 - GEN 11 & 12/ Y2 - 2 CHRON 5 & 6

Genesis 1:1-2 (NKJV)
In the beginning God created the heavens and the earth. The earth was without form, and void; and darkness was on the face of the deep. And the Spirit of God was hovering over the face of the waters.

The word for God in the Hebrew is Elohim, meaning creator. God chose to inform us within the first two chapters of His Word that we were created; I believe He wanted to emphasise that we are no accident.

We see in our text that God can create where there is a void. David tells us, **'The heavens declare the glory of God and the firmament shows his handiwork (Psalms 19:1 NKJV).'** Elohim (our creator) is in no way restricted. When David royally messed up with Bathsheba, he cried out to God saying, **'Create in me a clean heart and renew a steadfast spirit within me (Psalms 51:10 NKJV).'** He recognised there was a black hole in his life and concluded that the solution was to call upon the ultimate creator to make something new.

2 Corinthians 5:17 (NKJV) Therefore, if anyone is in Christ, he is a new creation...

What is there in your life that is missing or something that you have never had?

When God created the heavens and the earth, He looked and declared that it was good; everything is made for His glory. Allow God to create for you, in you, and through you, so that He may be glorified.

If you want God to create something in your life:

1) Speak words of faith through and with prayer.

2) Connect with the Spirit; be sensitive to Him and know His works and abilities.

3) Believe in your creator. His desire is to be glorified in you.

January 9th – *Famous Four*
Y1 - GEN 13 & 14 / Y2 - 2 CHRON 7 & 8

Daniel 3:24-25 (NIV)
Then King Nebuchadnezzar leaped to his feet in amazement and asked his advisers, "Weren't there three men that we tied up and threw into the fire?" They replied, "Certainly, Your Majesty." He said, "Look! I see four men walking around in the fire, unbound and unharmed, and the fourth looks like a son of the gods."

In the book of Daniel, when Shadrach, Meshach, and Abednego went into the flames, they trusted God would be with them, and He was! King Nebuchadnezzar saw that there were 4 men in the furnace because Jesus was right there with them in the midst of their trial. Jesus did not stand outside and watch, allowing them to fend for themselves, He got right in there with them and sheltered them from harm. God chose to reveal himself in the flesh to bring protection to three faithful servants. Regardless of what you are going through right now, Jesus promises to be with you also.

Deuteronomy 31:8 (NLT)
Do not be afraid or discouraged, for the Lord will personally go ahead of you. He will be with you; he will neither fail you nor abandon you.

The definition of being abandoned is desertion without the intention of returning, leaving the person or thing helpless without protection.[1] It's easy to feel lonely and perhaps even abandoned when you've been launched out of the mother church to pioneer a new work. We are away from loved ones and in unfamiliar surroundings. But God reassures us that He is always by our side. We do not have to feel neglected when we do not see or feel God. Rest assured that Jesus stays close to you wherever you are. Amongst friends or enemies, Christ sticks close to you. During our trials, God gets stuck in the midst and stands with us in the fiery furnaces of life.

January 10th – *Friend Machine*
Y1 - GEN 15 & 16 / Y2 - 2 CHRON 9 & 10

1 Samuel 18:1 (NKJV)
Now when he had finished speaking to Saul, the soul of Johnathan (Saul's son) was knit to the soul of David, and Johnathan loved him as his own soul.

Johnathon and David were besties, mates, and brothers. I don't know about you, but I wasn't prepared for the shift in my relationships when we moved to another city. For months I couldn't comprehend why only a couple of friends had called me, let alone visit. I thought I was 'close' to many, but now it seemed that no one cared; I felt hurt and alone. Didn't anyone understand what I was going through?

My thoughts eventually started to come together, and some rationale kicked in when I shared my heart with Jesus. Wasn't it I that chose to leave? Were my expectations too high? Was it self-pity that I was feeling?

'Friendship' is a broad-spectrum term and includes fellow pastor's wives, work colleagues, school mums, and ladies in church. But as we mature, 'best friends' like David and Johnathon are few and that is something we must accept. It is so incredibly important to maintain long term, spiritual, sisterly friendships. These are the type you trust, the type that keep you accountable, and the type that keep you topped up with spiritual words of encouragement. *Can you name these women in your life?*

John 15:15 "...But I have called you friends..."

Many of us came to Jesus empty handed, but he offered a hand of friendship. Jesus shows us that there are no conditions, bias, or prejudice attached to offering a hand of friendship. Wisdom is needed, but I'm sure you will agree that it is people that bring immense colour to life.

John 13:15 "For I have given you an example, that you should do as I have done."

You have the capacity to be a great friend, to offer support, love, and ultimately Jesus. I encourage you, be the friend machine that God has called every one of us to be.

January 11th – *No Partiality*
Y1 - GEN 17 & 18 / Y2 - 2 CHRON 11 & 12

James 2:9 (NKJV)
"but if you show partiality, you commit sin, and are convicted by the law as transgressors."

We went into a very big city with a complete diverse culture to pioneer a new work. The area our mother church was in was quite singular in culture at the time. Once we moved, we were surrounded by many cultures which neither my husband nor I had experienced on such a scale. Through conversation and fellowship, I showed the people in our congregation the same grace, love, and forgiveness that my pastor's wife had shown me, regardless of race or other factors. I learned that this is really all people want and need. As our husbands preach and raise up disciples, our calling or ministry as the wife is to show God's attributes, thus allowing people to grow to their full potential in God. When we treat all people with the same love and respect it allows them the freedom which they might not have experienced before coming to church.

Acts 10:34-35 (NKJV)
"Then Peter opened his mouth and said: "In truth I perceive that God shows no partiality. But in every nation whoever fears Him and works righteousness is accepted by Him."

One of the greatest temptations for a pastor's wife is to endorse segregation or second-class citizens in church. The longer you are in the ministry the more you will find yourself tested by the variety and diversity of God's people. We must make a conscious effort and decision to prevent this from creeping into our heart or church culture.

Romans 11:6 (NKJV)
"And if by grace, then it is no longer of works; otherwise grace is no longer grace..."

This scripture teaches us it is all about grace. God gives and shows us grace, and it is never about works. As pastor's wives we need to show this by example to those in our congregations.

January 12th – *Living Now*
Y1 - GEN 19 & 20 / Y2 - 2 CHRON 13 & 14

John 4:35 (NKJV)
Do you not say, 'There are still four months and *then* comes the harvest'? Behold, I say to you, lift up your eyes and look at the fields, for they are already white for harvest!

We are pioneering a church, and whilst in its infancy, I find myself looking to the future. How many people will come? What will the congregation be like? What kind of atmosphere or culture will the church have? Asking these questions is not a problem in itself, but I have felt like things were holding our ministry back and I realised that my thought patterns were like this:

When the church grows, we can...
When we have a building, we can...
When the Covid-19 pandemic passes, we can...

One Sunday, I was observing our service with dissatisfaction and God prompted me to remember that our <u>ministry does not begin when life starts to run more smoothly</u>; it starts with the young man who has been attending our Covid-19 online living room church services faithfully.

Things might be different 'when the kids are grown' or 'when we have a church building,' but our ministry is the here and now! It is nice to imagine that we will have a tight knit church with a culture of fellowship, love, and support. However, that has to start in the now, with us demonstrating that kind of culture already with the ones and twos that are coming through the door today.

Lord, thank you for the life that you have given me and for the here and now. I know that tomorrow isn't promised, but I also know that you will not leave me nor forsake me. Help me to do the best that I can with the resources I have now, and though I might look to the future, let that not distract me from the present. Amen.

January 13th - *Testimony*

Y1 - PS 3 / Y2 - PS 107

My Dream by Coral

My husband first went to the Fiji Islands in 1992 with an impact team from our church in Wollongong, Australia. He came back excited and stirred about what God was doing there and he felt like this was where God was leading him. He'd had a yearning for the islands ever since he was a young boy. Soon after, he took me to Fiji to see it myself and it was honestly the worst trip ever! However, I knew that God wanted us there.

In the days and weeks after the trip, my husband would say to me, "Are you ready to go?" I would answer him by saying, "When God speaks to me, I'll go." This of course was a very careless approach to the will of God, but I was full of insecurities and questions about going overseas with a family; concerned about things like education, health facilities, and disease. On one hand, I was saying that I trusted God with our lives and future, but on the other I was making, what sounded like, reasonable excuses before God. My husband continued to ask me about the mission field, but I persisted with the usual answer, "God will let us know when it's time."

<u>The Dream</u>

One-night God gave me a dream that I was walking along the beachfront esplanade in Wollongong and carrying my handbag, which happened to be full of money. I saw a commotion down at the water's edge, a young boy and girl crying out for help. They were looking out to the ocean and frantically yelling for someone to save their sister who was drowning. The beach was full of people and no one was taking any notice of their cries. I immediately jumped in the ocean holding my handbag (I couldn't leave it on the beach because I feared it would be stolen) and swam out to the little girl. I tried to grab her outstretched hand, but my bag, pulled me back and I missed. She surfaced again and I stretched out my hand to her, our fingers nearly touching, but still I couldn't grab hold. I knew it was my bag that was holding me back; I knew if I let go of my bag, it would be gone forever, but I would be able to reach that bit further and save the little girl. She was surfacing for what I knew in my heart was the last time, so I let go of the bag and was able to grasp her hand. The joy unspeakable of saving her replaced the loss of the bag. I swam back in with the little girl and placed her in the arms of her very thankful brother and sister. I stepped back and watched the rejoicing and the crowd gathering. As I turned around, there on a rock was my bag! I ran over to it, crying out, "It's a miracle!" Not only was everything in my bag still intact but, right beside it, was a large pile of money.

When I woke up in the morning, I knew it was a God given dream. I relayed it to my husband and he also felt it was from God. I knew I had to let go of my insecurities and put my trust in God. I felt God was promising that if I let go, He would give me the true riches. I told my husband, "I'll go anywhere in the world you want to go!" And now I can attest there is no greater joy than seeing souls saved while God takes care of you and your family.

Mat 19:29 (NKJV)
"And everyone who has left houses or brothers or sisters or father or mother or wife or children or lands, for My name's sake, shall receive a hundredfold, and inherit eternal life".

January 14th - *Study & Sermon notes*

Y1 - PS 4 / Y2 - PS 108

January 15th – *Sure Belief*

Y1 - GEN 21 & 22 / Y2 - 2 CHRON 15 & 16

James 1:6 (NKJV)
But let him ask in faith, with no doubting, for he who doubts is like a wave of the sea driven and tossed by the wind.

Going back into our mother church after being out pastoring was, at first, a great mental challenge. I was full of doubt that it was God's will and we were where we were supposed to be; doubting God's promises for the future and His infinite wisdom.

This doubt left me with a storm raging within me. A storm of confusion, unable to find rest because my refuge was the very thing I was doubting. Gripped by fear for the future and exhausted, I was desperate to find rest in a place that had become unfamiliar. The mother church had moved on and I was wondering how I would 'fit in.' I was unstable, wavering, feeling bruised, like being tossed in the wind.

During this rollercoaster of emotions, God gave me a revelation; when we doubt, we are not standing on God's Word with His victory, instead we make ourselves victims! God calls for us to ask in faith, without doubt. Doubt causes an uncertainty in God's goodness. Doubt shows a lack of faith, just like the disciples did in the boat.

Matthew 14:31 NKJV
And immediately Jesus stretched out His hand and caught him, and said to him, 'O you of little faith, why did you doubt?'

It is only when we fully surrender and believe in the promises of God and that His Word stands forever, that God can give us peace and calm our storm. I had to ask with a sure belief and then He came through and calmed the storm within.

There will always be storms in life, trials to face, adjustments to be made, but it is God's purpose to use every circumstance to change us into the people that He wants us to be.

January 16th – *Placenta Cream*
Y1 - GEN 23 & 24 / Y2 - 2 CHRON 17 & 18

Isaiah 5:21 NLT
What sorrow for those who are wise in their own eyes and think themselves so clever.

I was so excited to be given one of the most exclusive face creams on the market. It was expensive and hard to source; that's all I needed to know as I smugly smeared it on my face each night. After a few weeks I decided to look at the exclusive ingredients and I was horrified to read it contained placenta. Yes, I had been smearing the remnants of someone's placenta on my face. When I told my husband about the source of my beauty, his reaction of disgust was so funny I nearly hyperventilated laughing; you just had to be there.

The longer we are saved and serve in the ministry, we can begin to think we know it all, that we've seen it all, and that we are beyond needing to learn. This can be slyly hidden behind a listening ear with all the right answers, a tut at the latest misdemeanours of a new convert, or a smile at the leaders' blunder. You have elevated yourself to a place of wisdom whereby you think God himself struggles to find your faults.

Proverbs 31:30 NLT
Charm is deceptive, and beauty does not last; but a woman who fears the LORD will be greatly praised.

This verse is reminding us to look deeper if we want to obtain something more valuable. Charm and beauty are like passing vapours; we chase them and perhaps achieve them, but as quickly as they come, they go. I had the latest recommended beauty cream thinking it would make me stunning but instead it caused disgust. We may look and feel wise or beautiful in the world's eyes (or at least our own), but we need to focus on what God sees as important. Fear the Lord first and foremost, then you will have something of more value, both Godly wisdom and beauty.

January 17th – *Church Yes!*
Y1 - GEN 25 & 26 / Y2 - 2 CHRON 19 & 20

Hebrews 10:25 NIV
"not giving up meeting together, as some are in the habit of doing, but encouraging one another-and all the more as you see the Day approaching."

There was a phase in America a few years ago where people started buying bumper stickers saying, 'Jesus, yes! Church, No!' I believe that the world no longer understands the true value and power of the local church; *what about you? Do you see the value in your labour of love regarding the church?*

Funnily enough, I think that the concept of church runs parallel to Slimming World; it will change lives if people attend meetings and respond to 'the call.' Slimming World offers the overweight person (the sinner) the opportunity to make a change and lose weight (repent). It offers you a new family that will support you in this journey alongside those that are wiser and more experienced (congregation/fellowship). You get the chance to 'weigh in' every week (attend church/check yourself) and hear a special message from the leader (sermon from the pastor) that will educate, encourage, and compel you to keep going in this new found mission.

There is, however, a major difference between Slimming World and the church and it is this: Slimming World was Margaret Miles-Bramwell's idea but The Church was God's, it is not a man-made concept! Faithfully attending <u>one</u> church is the will of God and indeed, a place (like no other) where we experience His ministering presence.

The local church is a spiritual engine that encourages, produces friendships, strengthens marriages, makes disciples, inspires ministries, creates community, fulfills God's purpose of world evangelism, and so much more. Without God using a pastor and his wife building the church, the world today would be unrecognisable; by the grace of God we are the vessels He uses to serve in this capacity.

It is of the utmost importance to attend church; without church people rarely 'make it' for God. Just bare this in mind when getting up early on Sundays to prepare lunch for new converts, practise piano, or prepare for Sunday School. We do this together, side by side, not for a religious organization, but for the glory of our King.

January 18th – *God Sings*
Y1 - GEN 27 & 28 / Y2 - 2 CHRON 21 & 22

Zephaniah 3:17 (NIV)
The LORD your God is with you, the Mighty Warrior who saves. He will take great delight in you; in his love he will no longer rebuke you but will rejoice over you with singing.

What an interesting way to see one of the great many attributes of God!

Have you ever considered that God could rejoice over us with singing?

It seems like such a human attribute; I never really imagined the Almighty God singing, but then I suppose if we're made in His image and enjoy music and singing as much as we do, how much more the entity that created it?

When we read this scripture in Zephaniah, we find that God loves to sing. The prophet draws a picture with his words which describes God as a musician who loves to sing for and with His children. Think about these words, 'He will take great delight in you...will rejoice over you with singing.' To imagine God so filled with delight that it would cause Him to sing is such a fascinating thought! We know how it feels to suddenly burst into song because of emotion evoked from joy or a lament borne out of a disappointing or painful experience. We've experienced a song stuck in our head that helps us stay upbeat throughout the day. Now imagine God's voice booming out a song of praise for His children; *what would it sound like?*

I look forward to the day when we'll be together with God alongside all those who've put their trust in Jesus as their Saviour. How amazing it will be to hear our heavenly Father sing songs for and with us and experience His love, approval, and acceptance. How exciting!

Thank you, Jesus, for music and singing. Help me to love and prioritise praising you. Amen.

January 19ᵗʰ – *Conquering Intimidation*

Y1 - GEN 29 & 30/ Y2 - 2 Chron 23 & 24

Deuteronomy 31:6 (MSG)
"Be strong. Take courage. Don't be intimidated. Don't give them a second thought because GOD, your GOD, is striding ahead of you. He's right there with you. He won't let you down; he won't leave you."

My husband and I were announced to take over a church. We were so excited for all God was going to do, however, deep down, I felt so inadequate and ill equipped. The previous Pastor's wife was so lovely, although we were very different people, I felt I had to be like her. The women of the church, in my eyes, were so spiritually strong and full on, which in comparison I am not (I happily describe myself as God fearing, straightforward, and down to earth). I didn't feel worthy enough to be their Pastor's wife and honestly felt intimidated by them.

I didn't let fear and intimidation stop me. I served, built relationships, and did what I knew to do. After a while, God began to reveal how superficial some of those members were. I realised I had been intimidated by a façade. The areas in which I thought I lacked, God revealed to me that I didn't. He had equipped me with wisdom, knowledge, and a strong foundation.

We allow ourselves to doubt what God is doing, doubt our capabilities, and be intimidated by what He has put before us. But God always knows what He is calling us to and He promises to walk with us every step of the way. In times of intimidation, God gives us a strength that we do not possess in ourselves.

Lord, forgive me for doubting the work that you have done in me. Help me be strong and courageous; to not let fear and intimidation rule my thoughts, feelings, and actions. I know You go before me and will never let me down. Amen

January 20th - *Testimony*

Y1 - PS 5 / Y2 - PS 109

Overcoming Fear by Sarah

2Timothy1:7 (NKJV)
"For God has not given us a spirit of fear, but of power and of love and of a sound mind."

The funny thing is I never suffered with fear until I got saved, or at least I didn't notice it.

I can't really tell you when I started to feel so scared, but I never felt comfortable alone. I never told anyone because I didn't think it was a big deal. I thought that when I got married, I would get over it, but I soon realised marriage wasn't the cure. When my husband left the house for work, I would jump out of bed and be out the door five minutes after him. I would come home five minutes before him and do a quick clean up before he walked through the door, so it looked like I had been home all day.

I hate to admit this, but I was bound and living in this state for three years. I would go to people's houses, hang around the town; anything but be in a house by myself. A couple of times I would try to be brave and stay home, but it always got the better of me and I would run.

Until I heard a sermon on the Spirit of Fear. 'Oh no,' I thought, 'I have a spirit?' That night I confessed all to my husband. He was so shocked because he had no idea how extreme the situation had become. I knew I needed freedom from this, enough was enough! My husband laid hands on my head and started praying, that's all I remember. When I came around, to my surprise, I was on top of the kitchen counter. My husband's eyes were the size of saucers and he looked scared to death.

I asked him, "How did I get up here? What happened?" He calmly replied, "You definitely had a spirit, but it's gone now!"

Wow! I felt like a new person, I had clarity in my mind and peace.

I would love to tell you that is the end of my story and that I have been free ever since, but unfortunately that would not be true. It has been a long and hard battle to remain free. Making myself stay home, I would say my list of scriptures repeatedly.

Today, however, I am free from fear, God has been so faithful to me. I have learned to rely on God and His Word.

Joshua 1:9 (ESV- capitals added) "Have I not COMMANDED you? Be strong and courageous. Do not be frightened, and do not be dismayed, for the LORD your God is with you wherever you go."

Fears are very real, especially in the crazy times we are living in. You don't have to be bound by fear though, you can overcome it by relying on scripture and trusting in God.

January 21st - *Study & Sermon notes*

Y1 - PS 6 / Y2 - PS 110

January 22nd – *Role Model*
Y1 - GEN 31 & 32 / Y2 - 2 CHRON 25 & 26

Titus 2:3B (MSG)
Guide older women into the lives of reverence so they end up neither as gossips nor drunks, but models of goodness. By looking at them, the younger women will know how to love their husbands and children, be virtuous and pure, keep a good house, be good wives. We do not want anyone looking down on God's message because of their behaviour.

The phrase 'Do as I say, not do as I do' directly contradicts the Christian life because being an example is paramount.

The Pastor's wife, whether she accepts it or not, is an example; the choice to be a good, reverent one, is up to her. Your position means that your conduct is constantly being observed and used as a reference point for men, women, and children.

How you treat your husband and children, your words, facial expression, temperament, modesty, buying habits, willingness to be inconvenienced and serve, relationship with Jesus and His word, the way you discipline your children, your secular job, relationship with social media, and even the state of your house are all factors that people digest and use to paint a picture of who you are in Christ.

'I just speak my mind!' is another phrase that contradicts our conduct. Surely it is important to God for us to consider our words because we know that they affect people. If you will be especially careful in conduct you will gain favour with many people. A woman of integrity can be trusted, and her example will always be a reference point that brings glory to God.

Lord, I recognise the importance of my example. I ask you to help me to be aware of myself. Give me confidence to be and do the right thing. Show me how to change and equip me to thrive in Your will for Your glory and furtherance of the Kingdom.

January 23rd – *Smelly Onions*
Y1 - GEN 33 & 34 / Y2 - 2 CHRON 27 & 28

Deuteronomy 4:29 (NLT)
And if you search for him with all your heart and soul, you will find him.

A famous Shrek line says, 'Onions have layers!' We are just like onions, the deeper into our relationship with Christ, the stronger we get. The ripest foods always have the strongest flavour. I love a couple of black bananas; don't they make the best banana bread!

Although I don't think Jesus would want us to turn green and furry like a well aged cheese, He would definitely want us to be the strongest, most mature Christians that we can be. Take the 'title' of Pastor's wife away, Christ just wants us to be good Christians, loving God, loving people, reading our bibles, submitting in prayer, sharing the gospel, and discipling people in Christ. But with all the expectations and pressures of being an example, it's easy to make being in ministry complicated. These complications can cloud over the fundamental reason as to why we are on the harvest field in the first place. Jesus first loved us, and we loved Him in return, dedicating our lives in service.

Ask yourself these questions: *Are you praying? Are you reading the Word? Have you spoken to someone recently about Christ (Not three months ago, I mean recently)?* When God sees that we are seeking Him, He gives us His strength. I have spent a lot of time relying on my own strength only to give up and wonder, 'Why on earth did this not work out as I had planned?' Well, because I was relying on me. God gives us His strength when we fully trust and rely on His capabilities rather than our own.

Matthew 19:26 (NKJV)
But Jesus looked at *them* and said to them, 'With men this is impossible, but with God all things are possible.'

Let's strive to be mature Christians, making us the smelliest onions, the blackest bananas, and the most green and furry cheese we can be. Permission to use this only as an analogy and not neglect personal hygiene!

January 24th – *Handling Criticism*
Y1 - GEN 35 & 36 / Y2 - 2 CHRON 29 & 30

Luke 19:5-10 (NKJV)
And when Jesus came to the place, He looked up and saw him, and said to him, "Zacchaeus, make haste and come down, for today I must stay at your house." So, he made haste and came down, and received Him joyfully. But when they saw it, they all complained, saying, "He has gone to be a guest with a man who is a sinner." Then Zacchaeus stood and said to the Lord, "Look, Lord, I give half of my goods to the poor; and if I have taken anything from anyone by false accusation, I restore fourfold." And Jesus said to him, "Today salvation has come to this house, because he also is a son of Abraham; for the Son of Man has come to seek and to save that which was lost."

Here, the people complained about what Jesus has done; they don't approve of His decision and so began to criticize. Jesus does not justify His action, instead He communicates to Zacchaeus while they are listening and then educates them by using a parable. Jesus didn't get defensive but discerns that they need a righteous example and takes the opportunity to educate them.

Have you ever been or felt criticised?

Being the pastor's wife can naturally put us in the firing line for criticism, complaints, and questioning. Sometimes words are spoken to us from a kind heart and sometimes from a negative or unrighteous heart. While I'm sure you are aware that you are entitled to your own opinions, decisions, and privacy, simply having the confidence to navigate interrogative conversations can be difficult. When people impart little nuggets of 'wisdom' you must learn to chew on the meat and spit out the bones. Try not to get hung up on these situations. Whilst Satan wants you to dwell on them, Jesus wants you to grow from them and thrive. Keep your heart right, pray about it, and let God work out the rest.

January 25th – *Words Fail*
Y1 - GEN 37 & 38/ Y2 - 2 CHRON 31 & 32

Job 40:3 (MSG)
Job answered: 'I'm speechless, in awe—words fail me.'

The phrase 'words fail' describes a moment when the flow of speech that forms our communication has dried up and the cognitive mind is unable to process thoughts and produce words from them. You have no quick or witty comeback, no words to comfort, correct, pray, praise, or petition. In other words, you don't know what to say. We've all had those moments! Genesis tells us that God spoke the world into existence and that we are made in the likeness of God. *So, why are we lost for words when faced with situations that are bigger than ourselves? And what should we do when we are at a loss for words?* There are times when life-giving words need to be spoken, but they are not because we don't know exactly what to say.

Exodus 4:12 (TLB)
Now go ahead and do as I tell you, for I will help you to speak well, and I will tell you what to say.

John 14:25 (NIV)
But the Advocate, the Holy Spirit, whom the Father will send in my name, will teach you all things and will remind you of everything I have said to you.

Here's the answer: When our words fail, God's words do not. To know God's word for yourself will equip you to have the right words. If you can diligently learn to internalise bible verses, your ability to think quickly and speak wisdom will greatly increase. This is one of the works of the Holy Spirit in our lives and we need to trust Him to help us. Speak (or write) words that edify, share personal testimonies, encourage someone by letting them know you are praying for them, give scriptures to one another; let your words be a tool to express God's love and reach others.

Dear Lord, help me to be a vessel that brings Your word to others, Amen.

January 26th – *Historical Women*

Y1 - GEN 39 & 40 / Y2 - 2 CHRON 33 & 34

Nelda Mitchell

Proverbs 31:28-29 (NKJV)
Her children rise up and call her blessed; Her husband also, and he praises her: "Many daughters have done well, but you excel them all."

Nelda met and married Wayman in 1953. After the sudden death of their first child Terry, they experienced a profound conversion by Jesus Christ that would alter the course of their lives. They responded to the call to ministry, and they pastored in 5 different churches. In January 1970 they assumed the pastorate of the small and struggling Foursquare Gospel Church in Prescott, AZ (later called The Potter's House). Shortly after they arrived, God began to reach large numbers of young people during what has become known as the Jesus People Movement, and today the fellowship consists of 2,800 churches throughout the world, preaching the gospel in every corner of the earth.

Nelda was known for her great character. She was strong, extremely humorous, and very loving. Many expect the wife of a Pastor to take on a secondary Pastorate role, but not sister Nelda. She hated public speaking (at any event). Some would assume from this, that she wasn't spiritual, but quite the contrary. Whilst she was not flashy and outspoken, she had a deep relationship with Jesus that was unwavering. Her children testify that all of their lives they witnessed her reading the bible and praying (sometimes even in the bathroom to escape her five children).

Her legacy, very simply, is her example. She was real, she had influence, and she gave practical instruction to young people, children and families. She often ministered behind the scenes; one of these being the nursery (dealing with all kinds of situations that children and parents bring) and it was through this expression that she showed people how to love the unlovely. She regularly (from her own pocket of small wages) was seen to quietly hand a new suit to a disciple in church, encouraging that man to do the will of God. She was careful with her words, teaching women that, 'A child will always live up to what you say they are.'

She loved her husband, and many have testified they aspired to have a relationship like theirs. Their children recall that they never saw their parents fight; Nelda and Wayman decided that it wasn't in the children's best interest. She was indispensable to her husband and her example utterly essential in the ministry. She left her home, family, and comfortable security to move with her husband to Perth, Western Australia to assume the pastorate there on 3 occasions: At age 47, 51, and in a time of crisis and great need, at the age of 74! These instances are subtle but most profound.

Nelda was once asked by a friend, 'Did you always want to be a pastor's wife?' She replied with her infectious laugh and cheeky smile by saying, 'No, Pastor Mitchell quit the ministry for 2 years because I complained so much. Those years were so miserable that I decided, of my own will, to be a pastor's wife and to follow my husband wherever God would take us.'

Sister Mitchell shows how a quiet life surrendered to God can make a great impact. She died on August 25, 2016 having touched multiple thousands of lives, in over 110 nations, a godly example wherever she went.

January 27th - *Testimony*

Y1 - PS 7 / Y2 - PS 111

Hearing Ability by Vicky

In 2005, my husband and I were asked to take over a church, and with great joy we embraced the opportunity. However, there was one problem, I was born deaf. I gradually gained the ability to speak and my hearing improved by the time I was four, but three months prior to answering the call I was registered completely deaf in both ears. I couldn't hear a thing. I couldn't hear my children laugh or cry, my husband speaking or preaching, the congregation singing, people praying, thunderstorms, cars on the road, the dog barking, the washing machine, people on the phone, or even the door opening and closing .

How could I possibly minister as the wife of a pastor in our new church? Well, my bible says that I can do all things through Christ who strengthens me, God will always make a way when there seems to be no way, we just have to put our trust in Him.

Ironically, I experienced some unique benefits to being deaf whilst on the field: 1) When I arranged to meet a new convert during the week for coffee, they rarely missed the fellowship because they couldn't call me to cancel (because I can't hear on the phone). 2) Our congregation really protected me; they made sure I was looked after and were always there to help me communicate. 3) When we had people over for dinner, I would sit in the middle of the table (a privileged position) so that I could lip read everyone as they spoke. 4) Reading became a big part of my life.

The world has classified me as disabled, but I know that with God I am enabled! I remain optimistic and grateful for all that God has given me. After a number of years in the ministry an opportunity arose for me to have the cochlear implant. This was a miracle because the clinic was local to us and one of the best hearing clinics in the UK. If we had stayed in our mother church this opportunity probably wouldn't have come about. When I had this life changing procedure, I realised I had been living a life in black and white and now it seemed as though everything had been coloured in. Prior to this operation, sounds were a slur and now they were sharp. I could hear a cough, a crisp wrapper, and indeed for the first time in my life the beautiful African, Jamaican, and East Midland accents that surrounded us.

In 2014, God re-directed us back to our mother church where my husband answered the call to evangelise. This meant that he would be away three out of four weeks of the month. This was a new challenge, but one I was more than willing to embrace because I knew God was on my side and He would enable me. I had decided within the first few years of my salvation that despite my problems I would release my husband into the will of God. So, when the call to evangelise arrived, I wasn't overwhelmed, I trusted God like I always had.

When I came back to the mother church, to my surprise, friends would comment on how I had changed. They said I had grown in confidence and strength. God had changed me through my experiences as a pastor's wife. I learnt to truly depend on my saviour instead of being consumed with fear.

Proverbs 3:5 (NKJV) Trust in the Lord with all your heart and lean not on your own understanding. In all your ways acknowledge him and he will direct your path.

This is my favourite scripture. Whilst my disability is a visible one, we all struggle with problems that can disable us internally, in our hearts. Let the Lord be your ever-present help in times of trouble and through Him you will be more than a conqueror.

January 28th - *Study & Sermon notes*

Y1 – PS 8 / Y2 - PS 112

....

....

....

....

....

....

....

....

....

....

....

....

....

....

....

....

....

....

January 29th – *Discerning Spirit*
Y1 - GEN 41 & 42 / Y2 - 2 CHRON 35 & 36

Philippians 1:9 (NKJV)
And this I pray, that your love may abound still more and more in knowledge and all discernment...

To discern is to see, recognise, or understand something that is not clear. Discernment is the ability to judge people and things well,[1] or to perceive.[2] Discernment can describe the process of determining God's desire in a situation or for one's life.[3] A discerning individual is considered to possess wisdom and insight.

John 7:24 (NKJV)
Do not judge according to appearance, but judge with righteous judgment.

Here Jesus is teaching that we should not judge superficially, for example; we had a man in our church who had been saved for eight years. He was head usher, dressed smartly for service, went on outreach, tithed, and would actively serve in the church. On the surface all looked well, but my husband and I felt uneasy about something, we just couldn't put our fingers on the root issue because it wasn't obvious. Then after some time, God revealed hidden immorality and had we ignored our sense that something was wrong, the church would have been further affected by his sin.

Ministry can be a relentless and often thankless task, but without discernment we can be working hard with no real results; people can end up using us and our good will. We need discernment in our walk with God as well as in so many other areas of life. There will be small decisions and major crossroads in which we must seek God's direction.

Pray that God would give you a discerning spirit and an ability to judge righteously. As God gives wisdom, He also can give discernment.

January 30th – *Losing Heart*
Y1 - GEN 43 & 44 / Y2 - 2 THES 1 & 2

2 Chronicles 25:2 (NLT)
Amaziah did what was pleasing in the LORD'S sight, but not wholeheartedly.

Every now and then, our cars need a service; and every now and then, our hearts need the same. We might be doing what is 'pleasing in the Lord's sight' without our hearts being engaged in the activity. Maybe we are doing right things (i.e. following-up on the new converts, serving the church by playing an instrument, volunteering in the church nursery, or perhaps it's simply making sure our families have dinner on the table at the end of the day), however, if we are really honest with ourselves, our hearts may just not be fully in it anymore. We're busy running around serving everyone else, but when we stop and take a look at ourselves, we might not be too 'wholehearted.'

The Holy Spirit is able to resurrect a fresh fire within us, which will then enable us to love God and serve Him wholeheartedly again.

Isaiah 42:3 (NLT) He will not crush the weakest reed or put out a flickering candle.

Philippians 1:6 (NIV) being confident of this, that he who began a good work in you will carry it on to completion until the day of Christ Jesus.

This has encouraged me many times. We are still a work in progress; we have a promise that He will continue working in us, and God can restore our hearts once more. Don't lose your fire. Whilst we may be busy serving others, let us not lose our own convictions or grow weary. Let's continue to pray, study God's Word, and keep our hearts set upon Him.

Self-care is giving the world the best of you, instead of what's left of you. — Katie Reed

January 31st – *Seeking Spirituality*

Y1 - GEN 45 & 46 / Y2 - 2 THES 3

1 Chronicles 16:11 (NKJV)
Seek the Lord and His strength; Seek His face evermore!

I was troubled when a friend of mine uttered the words, 'I'm not very spiritual.' Not only was she a Christian, but also the wife of a pastor. Here are a few connotations:

1. She feels inadequate because she is comparing herself to others.
2. Perhaps she lacks confidence.
3. She struggles or does not prioritise a relationship with God and therefore lacks a spiritual dimension to her life.

It is important to define Christian spirituality. 1 It is the conscious human response to God that is both personal and ecclesial; it is tuning into the Spirit. Regardless of the outflow of your Christianity, let it be said, in the very least, that you are seeking the mind of God and reading His Word daily. An act of spirituality is prioritising Jesus every day.

I fought for years to have a consistent prayer life and I would get so frustrated with myself; why couldn't I defeat the duvet demon? After pouring out my heart to a godly friend about my desperation to overcome this stumbling block, she instructed me to read (and digest) one chapter of the bible per day and pray, undisturbed; it took 15 minutes. The practicality of this approach set me free; sometimes you must go back to basics in order to rebuild. The result was I grew, became more sensitive to His voice, and felt more equipped to live life.

It is not 'ok' to remain the same as a Christian. God created living things to grow. You see other women being 'spiritual' and progressing in their faith and you say, 'that can never be me.' It can be you! It must be you! God's plan for you is unlimited so don't restrict yourself by analysing your abilities. It is God that enables us; seek His face continually and you will break through.

February 1st – *Constantly Adapting*

Y1 - GEN 47 & 48 / Y2 – EZRA 1 & 2

I Corinthians 9:19-23 (NKJV)
For though I am free from all men, I have made myself a servant to all, that I might win the more; and to the Jews I became as a Jew, that I might win Jews; to those who are under the law, as under the law, that I might win those who are under the law; to those who are without law, as without law (not being without law toward God, but under law toward Christ), that I might win those who are without law; to the weak I became as weak, that I might win the weak. I have become all things to all men, that I might by all means save some. Now this I do for the gospel's sake, that I may be partaker of it with you.

A major learning curve for me, personally, in the short time we've been pioneering is to be adaptable. God is constantly surprising us with what He will do next with this church. Our opening Sunday morning church service had 7 people, that evening 29!

Paul teaches us to 'become all things to all men' and I found this very difficult to begin with; my words would always be, 'this isn't how we did it in my mother church.' I had to adapt fast to what God was doing, stop comparing, and learn to relax in order for God to use me effectively. In our mother church, for example, the children are well-disciplined and there is a nursery, so the little ones aren't often heard during the service. When we first opened the church, we had an outpouring of souls attend, but with them came around eight children (age two and below), it was chaos. I had to adapt to children screaming, shouting, and running around while my husband was preaching, all without going crazy at the parents. I learnt to be patient and allow God to move and He has.

Are you able to adapt? God helped Paul, He can help you and me!

We can't stop the waves, but we can learn how to surf - Jon Kabat-Zinn

February 2nd – *Health Kick*
Y1 – GEN 49 & 50 / Y2 – EZRA 3 & 4

1 Timothy 4:8 (NKJV)
For bodily exercise profits a little, but godliness is profitable for all things, having promise of the life that now is and of that which is to come.

As a pastor's wife, it is so important that we keep our body and mind healthy. It's proven that physical exercise is essential for the health not only of the body, but of the mind. I know we can all struggle to fit this into our daily lives as we are so busy, but just taking 30 minutes out of your day, giving your children to your husband, and going for a walk, jog, or home workout will do you the world of good.

Maintaining physical wellbeing is essential, but more importantly, we can't neglect to prioritize our spiritual wellbeing. There are many reasons for our attention to turn to other aspects of life other than the spiritual, but we must make every effort to prioritise. Therefore, it is vital to be listening to sermons, reading books, and having spiritual conversations throughout the week. There is a plethora of sermons available online and I have found that since making time to listen, I have been so encouraged and blessed. They sustain me when I don't get to hear the sermon because I am taking care of my twin toddlers (Lord send nursery workers PLEASE!).

This is my challenge to you: make it a habit of listening to an additional sermon with good, biblical preaching once a week (maybe during your exercise time), read a new Christian book once a month, and call another pastor's wife or sister to have a chat which edifies and encourages one another.

It will help you, and others.

Father, I recognise my need to be well physically and spiritually. I ask you to highlight areas in my life that need attention. Please motivate me to put them right and see progression. Thank you, father, Amen.

February 3rd - *Testimony*

Y1 - PS 9 / Y2 – PS 113

Vanessa's Salvation Story

I was saved from a religious Catholic background in which I was taught how to memorise and recite different prayers but, I had never actually learnt how to pray. Shortly after I got saved, due to circumstances beyond our control, my roommates from church and I moved in with my pastor and his family temporarily. Whilst living with them, I got a personal revelation and started waking up every day for morning prayer meetings at church. At first, I had no idea what I was doing, so I would listen to my pastor pray and this is how I learnt to talk to God as my Father. I enjoyed my intimate moments with God and being single I had ample time to read my bible and study. This habit really helped me even after I got married, however, when I had children I was no longer able to go to morning prayer and with the busyness of young babies, I could never find time to spend with God like I used to.

I carried on functioning but became distracted by raising our children, ministry, and general life. I did not realise that I was just a ticking time bomb. We had two babies under two years old when we were sent out to take over a church. We hit the ground running. Now, in addition to a minimal prayer life, I was missing services because I had to do nursery. I was lacking spiritual input but was constantly giving out in serving my family and the ladies in church. It was at this point I experienced an overload and exploded. I was running on empty and could not go on. My husband was thriving, but I was overwhelmed and ultimately angry.

I remembered my pastor's wife always said, 'Check your heart.' And so, I did, and discovered that I was lost. I was busy doing everything else, but I had forgotten the most important thing, my relationship with God. I fell to my knees in repentance and asked God to forgive me. God challenged me to get up two hours earlier than everyone else in our house to pray and spend time with Him. For me that meant 5:00 a.m.; I set my alarm and began my journey back to intimacy with God. It wasn't easy, but as I was obedient in keeping my appointment with God, it absolutely transformed my life. Make prayer a priority in your life, you cannot give what you do not have.

February 4th - *Study & Sermon notes*

Y1 – PS 10 / Y2 – PS 114

February 5th – *Jehovah God*

Y1 – MATT 1 & 2 / Y2 -EZRA 5 & 6

Isaiah 43:10-11 (NKJV)
"You are My witnesses," says the LORD, "And My servant whom I have chosen, that you may know and believe Me and understand that I am He. Before Me there was no God formed, nor shall there be after Me. I, even I, am the LORD, and besides Me there is no saviour."

Jehovah is the most used name for God in the bible and translates to 'Lord'. 'LORD' (Jehovah) in capitals, is used to differentiate from 'Lord' (Adonai) in the KJV.[1]

Jehovah is derived from the Hebrew word havah, 'to be' or 'being'.[2] Strong's dictionary says, 'the existing one'.[3] He 'is' the same, yesterday, today, and forever (Hebrews 13:8). He doesn't change.

Exodus 34:5-7 (NKJV)
Now the LORD descended in the cloud and stood with him there, and proclaimed the name of the LORD. And the LORD passed before him and proclaimed, "The LORD, the LORD God, merciful and gracious, longsuffering, and abounding in goodness and truth, keeping mercy for thousands, forgiving iniquity and transgression and sin..."

As Jehovah, He brings judgement, yet also love; He is righteous and holy.[4] He is a God of covenant. His attributes do not change, His plan and purposes for our lives do not change, and His promises to us do not change.

Isaiah 45:24 (NKJV)
He shall say, "Surely in the LORD *[Jehovah]* I have righteousness and strength..."

As this scripture says, through Jehovah, we have salvation and strength. We aren't strong enough by ourselves to do His will or withstand trials and temptations. We must always remember to lean on Him!

Jehovah is such a powerful name of God and has so many aspects. Let's remember to worship and call on His name with gratitude, faith, and reverence. He is *I AM.*

February 6th – *Attack Anxiety*
Y1 – MATT 3 & 4 / Y2 -EZRA 7 & 8

There have been many times throughout my walk with Christ when I have felt anxious, fearful, and alone. When I became a Pastor's wife this intensified as I went through things I didn't understand and I began to experience panic attacks for the first time in my life. I had to learn the power scripture has to change my mindset, remind me who God is, and reassure me until my physical symptoms went away. Many scriptures gave me strength and comfort; here are two which I hope will bless and encourage you.

Isaiah 41:10 (NIV)
So do not fear, for I am with you; do not be dismayed, for I am your God. I will strengthen you and help you; I will uphold you with my righteous right hand.

Romans 8:38-39 (NIV)
I am convinced that neither death nor life, neither angels nor demons, neither the present nor the future, nor any powers, neither height nor depth, nor anything else in all creation, will be able to separate us from the love of God that is in Christ Jesus our Lord.

At my most vulnerable, I would read these verses every day, slowly reciting them, digesting every word, and putting my name in to make it personal: 'nothing can ever separate (me) from the love of God.' In time, I was able to quote the scripture by memory whenever I felt the anxiety rearing its ugly head. I would challenge my thoughts, quote the verse, 'He's upholding me with His righteous right hand,' and visualise His hand holding me. It led me to search the Bible for more scriptures and sometimes I would break out in praise at the revelation of what God promises. It was weeks after I embraced the power of scripture that the panic attacks actually stopped. I came to realise that scripture has the ability to bring change in the physical. Don't let the devil deceive you, God is there, He cares, and His Word has power!

February 7th – *Chilli Nut*

Y1 - MATT 5 & 6 / Y2 – EZRA 9 & 10

Romans 15:1-2 (NLT)
We who are strong must be considerate of those who are sensitive about things like this. We must not just please ourselves. We should help others do what is right and build them up in the Lord.

'Maybe he's hungry?' She thought whilst looking into the fish bowl. My little sister, age 5 at the time, had been eyeing my cousin's fish the entire day; all she wanted to do was pick it up and play with it! "He's definitely hungry, maybe he wants some of my chilli nuts." She reached into the packet, pulled out a couple and threw them into the bowl...It's safe to say that Ludvig the fish didn't survive the spicy snack and unfortunately died the next day. It was all very sad.

When a visitor walks into church, without doubt, excitement kicks in, especially if they respond to the invitation to receive Christ. Someone NEW, hallelujah! These are now little babes in Christ, and just like Ludvig, there are some things they just can't digest yet! The Bible says, they are to drink milk, and are not ready for meat. If we feed them more spiritual food than they can handle they could spiritually choke to death. "Why not come to our 3 weekly services and bible study? Did you know we have outreach every Saturday? Have you heard of tithing? Baptism? The Rapture? You better get rid of your sinful habits and pray everyday. Oh, and how was your first service at church?"

Now of course, this example is extreme, but we need to be wise with how we handle our new converts. It's often best not to answer questions that they haven't asked, leave that to God! He'll speak to them through the preaching and whilst they're praying and reading their bibles. God was powerful enough to save them, He's powerful enough to help them grow too! Keep a careful and loving eye on the bowl for when they need you, but no more chilli nuts!

February 8th – *Lady Disciple*
Y1 - MATT 7 & 8 / Y2 - 1 TIM 1 & 2

Matthew 27:55-56 (NIV)
Many women were there, watching from a distance. They had followed Jesus from Galilee to care for his needs. Among them were Mary Magdalene, Mary the mother of James and Joseph, and the mother of Zebedee's sons.

A disciple is simply 'a follower of Jesus.' This entails building a personal relationship with Him, adopting His character, and actively aligning your will to His. If you are a Christian, you are called to be a disciple. A disciple has a vision for the church and for the furtherance of the gospel. They feel the burden for the lost and a desire to evangelise. A disciple is willing to invest in people and love others as they love themselves. They will give themselves to prayer, fasting, and reading the Word. They sacrifice their time, money, and resources. They hunger for more of Jesus in their lives and work hard to prioritise Him from day to day. They bear their cross.

Are you a disciple?

The problem is, all too often, women subconsciously get caught up with rhetoric. We often hear 'men' referenced in the bible and over the pulpit because there is, rightly so, an emphasis on 'men' being called to preach, lead, and build a church. However, some women can unknowingly consider their husband as the 'disciple' rather than themselves. But regardless of gender, if you follow Jesus and live accordingly, you are a disciple.

We must put aside the concept that discipleship is for men only. The women in our text followed and cared for Jesus until His death and they postured themselves to serve Him. A perfect picture of discipleship. To serve is a matter of obedience, 'Lord, what do you want me to do?'

These women found themselves in the middle of the most important events of human history because they were followers of Jesus. We don't know where He will lead us, but He promises that we will never walk alone. It is surely the greatest life you could ever lead.

February 9th – *Personal Words*
Y1 - MATT 9 & 10/ Y2 - 1 TIM 3 & 4

Psalm 119:105 (NIV)
Your word is a lamp for my feet, a light on my path.

God is always wanting to speak to us. The problem is, He often can't be heard through the noise of our busy lives. God can speak to you personally, in that still small voice, through the Word of God, prophesy, or through the preaching. I've written in my bible on almost every blank page the dates when God spoke to me. I have a separate page for some of the prophecies that were given to me; I have highlighted scriptures with dates, have a page for quotes from sermons and preachers and I take notes during sermons to assist my concentration. Some of my friends keep journals, but whatever method you prefer, it is a necessity to record and recall when and what God has spoken to you.

About a year after my salvation, while at the altar during a conference repenting for putting my ambitions before God, I felt that God instructed me not to apply to college. I returned home, but still decided to apply, just in case I did not hear correctly! I found myself 6 months into the course, missing church, my heart turning away from Christ and being dazzled by the career prospects. I was lacking peace and unable to sleep. I picked up my Bible, opened it and read Deuteronomy 28:15-47 and God spoke to me very clearly! I then had to go through the embarrassing and humbling process of stopping the course (I'm not saying God is against college, this was His word to me and my situation).

When you cannot see any hope in a situation, when your life is not aligning with your dreams, or when you are discouraged and your faith is low, encourage yourself in the personal words, prophecies and promises that you've been given. The Bible says we have to work out our own (personal) salvation with fear and trembling. Record, apply and reflect upon God's promises to you.

February 10th - *Testimony*

Y1 – PS 11 / Y2 - PS 115

Missionary Guide by Claire

Isaiah 54:13 (NKJV)
All your children *shall be* taught by the Lord, and great *shall be* the peace of your children.

This was the scripture God gave me before leaving for China. I had been anxious that the education of my three sons would suffer in an unknown country with a language barrier. I pleaded with God not to make me home school, as I knew how much I'd struggle. We left for China with suitcases, a guitar, and a God given assurance that He would make a way. We did not know a soul in the City we were moving to, but when we arrived at the airport there were a bunch of students holding a banner saying, 'Welcome the... family'.

How did *that* happen? The night before we left, I received a phone call from a Chinese girl named Sally. She was a student, I had met in my mother church whilst preparing to leave and she was from the city we were going to! She had called to inquire about our flight details and arranged for some of her friends to meet us at the airport when we arrived. Amazing! From then on it was like 'walking on water' as God opened doors and guided us; an incredible experience.

Apart from my eldest son having to complete his GCSEs as a home-schooling program, our children have always attended wonderful schools and had great experiences. God also made a way for them to attend a Chinese school that ran a Canadian programme for higher education. My husband works for the school in exchange for the fees, and the bonus is, it gives us our visa to remain here to build God's church. All three of my children speak Chinese and their skill to communicate has been an incredible advantage to the Kingdom of God. God has always guided us!

February 11th - *Study & Sermon notes*

Y1 - PS 12 / Y2 - PS 116

February 12ᵗʰ – *He Answered*

Y1 - MATT 11 & 12 / Y2 - 1 TIM 5 & 6

Matthew 27:12-14 (NKJV)
And while He was being accused by the chief priest and elders, He answered nothing. Then Pilate said to Him, 'Do you not hear how many things they testify against You?' But He answered him not one word, so that the governor marvelled greatly.

As women of God, we are called to be peacemakers and work with a lot of different people, many times difficult people! It's easy to be misunderstood and be accused of things we have not said or done. In such moments, everything within our souls wants to put things right so that people in our congregation can see that we are innocent and have done nothing wrong.

Jesus stood before Pilate, innocent. Our text says, 'He answered him not a word, so that the governor marvelled greatly.' What an incredible example our Lord Jesus shows us! When everything within you wants revenge and judgement, 'answer not a word' and give it all to God! Let God put things right and heal your relationships. He is our defender. He is able, my friend!

Psalms 18:2 (NIV)
The LORD is my rock, my fortress and my deliverer; my God is my rock, in whom I take refuge, my shield and the horn of my salvation, my stronghold.

By your words and actions as a woman of God, many will see, marvel, and follow your example. How many of us have come to somebody with an issue and their soft and wise answer has made us change our hearts? That gentle spirit that answered nothing, in the midst of accusations, is God's own Spirit that is fully able to convict and change lives.

Lord Jesus, thank you for being a perfect example in times of trials and accusations. Fill me Lord with your Holy Spirit and give me wisdom in dealing with difficult people and difficult situations. Guard my emotions Lord and guard my tongue so that Your name will be magnified. Help me to be a peacemaker and an example. Give me a heart of forgiveness as you forgive me. Amen.

February 13th – *Child Training*
Y1 - MATT 13 & 14 / Y2 - 2 TIM 1 & 2

Proverbs 22: 6 (KJV)
Train up a child in the way he should go: and when he is old, he will not depart from it.

This verse is about more than just bible lessons at home, it is godly instruction woven into the daily activities of life. This is going to require a unique approach when in ministry, because your kids can have a lot more exposure to children who are disadvantaged, have no moral grounding, come from a chaotic home environment, or have parents that do not enforce boundaries. We have to reach these people whilst following biblical wisdom of how we raise our own children.

We have to teach our children to behave differently as our home environment is based on what God instructs. Some things that have helped me are the teachings through stories, using bible verses in a way they understand, and ensuring our home life lines up with biblical wisdom. Another element of this is talking to your children in an age appropriate way about what happens when individuals don't follow God's instruction.

Create a home environment of love and grace which allows your children to ask questions. Be honest about the need for their own salvation and relationship with God and emphasize the benefits of Godly instruction and wisdom in their life. Through boundaries, discipline, and love, your children will be set apart. This will give them the solid foundation to follow the Lord in years to come.

My Father, I put my children in Your hands and ask you to work in them. Help me to be a godly mother, an example in all my actions and words. Let them see You in me and feel Your grace and love in our home. Amen

February 14th – *Prayer Covering*
Y1 - MATT 15 & 16 / Y2 - 2 TIM 3 & 4

1 Corinthians 11:3 (NKJV)
But I want you to know that the head of every man is Christ, the head of woman is man, and the head of Christ is God.

As Pastor's wives we realise our husband's ministry has weight and is productive in God's Kingdom. We submit to our husband's authority, we might speak with our husband to gain wise counsel, *but do we ask him to pray for us?* Our husband is our covering, our authority, and head. I'm sure your husband will already be praying for you, but *does he know the areas you might be struggling with emotionally or spiritually in which they might pray for you specifically? Do you utilise him as your prayer covering?*

I was working through a series of mind assaults and struggling to fight them in prayer and bible reading when my husband suggested that he pray for me. I noticed a big difference and improvement, to say the least. I also noticed, from then onwards, that my husband would specifically cover my mind in prayer (as well as his usual prayers for me); this has been such a blessing.

1 Peter 3:7 (NIV)
Husbands, in the same way be considerate as you live with your wives, and treat them with respect as the weaker partner and as heirs with you of the gracious gift of life, so that nothing will hinder your prayers.

Peter is saying we are the weaker vessel; our husbands should look after us, treating us as something that is valuable or fragile.[1] Prayer is one amazing way our husbands can cover us, a way for us to come under them and a way for both of us to demonstrate surrender to God.

Lord, forgive me for underestimating the power and weight my husband has as my covering and headship. Help me to utilise his ministry and prayer life in the future. Amen.

February 15th – *Be Both*

Y1 - MATT 17 & 18 / Y2 – NEH 1 & 2

Romans 12:13 (NKJV)
Distributing to the needs of the saints, given to hospitality.

Our emphasis (and rightly so) is largely on reaching the lost, but in this verse, Paul speaks specifically about looking after those that serve in the church. He was urging church leaders and congregation members to open up their home and accommodate the visiting preachers, fellow believers, and dare I say the stranger. In new testament times, roads were incredibly dangerous, inns were very costly, scarce, and a place for sin. These were some of the reasons Paul urged believers to reach out.

The challenge is to be both types of people: *reach out to the lost and be hospitable to the saints.*

How can you practically incorporate serving into your life? Hospitable people are, more than likely, to burn out at some point. They feel the desperate need to reach people and keep serving. Sometimes all they need is a word of encouragement.

Bear in mind that seasons change and when they do, it's time to re-evaluate. Here are some tips:
- Speak to your husband every Sunday night and discuss the needs for the following week and how you can work together to meet them.
- Plan fellowships in advance (preferably at the beginning of the month, so it gives people enough notice).
- Be realistic.
- Budget for fellowships.
- Pray for God to show you needs and how to be creative in meeting those needs.

We are a family and together we can have an incredible impact throughout the world, but it doesn't mean we have to burn out. Many hands make light work.

Father, I ask you to give me a love for people, the sinner, and the saint. Help me to find a balance, that suits myself and my family, in order for me to avoid burnout. Show me when I need to re-evaluate and help me have an insight into every season. Amen

February 16th – *Name Drop*

Y1 - MATT 19 & 20 / Y2 - NEH 3 & 4

Philippians 2:9-11 (NKJV)
Therefore God also has highly exalted Him and given Him the name which is above every name, that at the name of Jesus every knee should bow, of those in heaven, and of those on earth, and of those under the earth, and *that* every tongue should confess that Jesus Christ *is* Lord, to the glory of God the Father.

A spirit had taken over my husband and he started to swear and insist he was going to the pub. After considerable time trying to convince him to sit and talk to me, it dawned on me that I could pray. I proclaimed the words, 'I cast all evil spirits out of my house in the name of Jesus!' I felt a push on my chest, a forceful wind blow across my mouth, and instantly I woke up. It was only a dream!

Of course, I felt rather unsettled when I awoke, but I was also overwhelmed by the power of the name of 'Jesus'. I know I've been guilty of throwing the phrase 'in the name of Jesus' around like a cliché, however, since this dream I have complete faith when I say this in prayer. 'I claim' or 'I cast out' is always followed by a heartfelt conviction of 'in the name of Jesus.'

When Paul explained the weight that the name of Jesus carries, he wasn't joking. Take a moment to consider, *are you guilty of using the name of Jesus as an empty comment? Do you understand the immense power in His name?* The words in our text, 'at the name of Jesus every knee shall bow' emphasises to us that by praying in His name He can bring anyone or anything to their knees in surrender.

Lord, help me to realise the capacity of Your wonderful name. You have blessed me with its authority, may I not take this for granted and use it foolishly, but delight in the power that You bring in the mighty name of Jesus. Amen

February 17th - *Testimony*

Y1 - PS 13 / Y2 - PS 117

Keeping Focus by Lisa

I was diagnosed with breast cancer in December 2011. It surprised me how something could rock my world completely; I had to re-evaluate everything and think about what was important to me. I couldn't sleep or settle for several nights, then my husband prayed for me and I had an encounter with God. I knew whatever happened, I was in God's hands and it was out of my control. I could sleep well again. I had to come to terms with the possibility of death, and although I knew I was going to heaven, it gave me a yearning for the people who weren't.

Soon after this I went, as usual, to outreach and met a lady who I led to salvation. I poured my life into her for about four weeks, speaking every day and meeting up constantly. During those times she would talk about everything going on in her very traumatic and difficult life. It was only when I had to have my mastectomy that I told her about my diagnosis. She couldn't believe I had been so caring and thoughtful, never mentioning the fact I had cancer. In truth, she helped me pull through that difficult time, because I had taken the focus off myself.

In 2013, while I was still undergoing multiple reconstruction operations, we were launched out to pioneer a church. Again, the focus on other people and keeping busy is what pulled me through. I knew the cancer had given me a new empathy and I could reach people I couldn't before because I had been through something so traumatic; my story was a testimony.

Cancer made me assess what is important in life: reaching souls, remaining heaven-bound, and my family. I had a peace and joy inside which many observed and recognised could only have come from God. Keeping the focus off myself, and on the things of God kept me going through the difficult times.

February 18th - *Study & Sermon notes*

Y1 - PS 14 / Y2 - PS 118

February 19th – *Why fast?*

Y1 - MATT 21 & 22 / Y2 – NEH 5 & 6

Matthew 6:16–18 (NIV)
When you fast, do not look somber as the hypocrites do, for they disfigure their faces to show others they are fasting. Truly I tell you, they have received their reward in full. But when you fast, put oil on your head and wash your face, so that it will not be obvious to others that you are fasting, but only to your Father, who is unseen; and your Father, who sees what is done in secret, will reward you.

Jesus says **when** you fast, not **if** you fast. Therefore, it is something He expects all Christians to do in whatever way they can. Fasting is not a religious duty, but it's something that comes from our heart and is private between you and God. No-one needs to know you are fasting. Unlike everything else we may 'do' in the name of serving God, this is a true revealer of where God is in our priorities.

Fasting is so much more than a withdrawal from food; it can be a time of separation from anything that distracts us from God. It's a way to regularly re-align ourselves back to Jesus in prayer so we can hear His voice, and a way of giving praise for what we have through salvation. Fasting is a time set aside for radically focusing on God. Denying our temporary pleasures means we can be more dependent on God for satisfaction.

Plan regularly when you are going to fast from food, as well as times of fasting from other pleasures. We should be willing to make this a priority because we love God more than anything else.

Prayer points:
- Pray that God reveals the possible idols in your heart that take away the focus from Jesus.
- Pray God will speak to you concerning His will for your life.
- Ask God to show you specific people and needs to target in prayer.
- Pray that God helps you experience His power through your times of private fasting.

February 20th – *Loudest Voice*
Y1 - MATT 23 & 24 / Y2 - NEH 7

Mark 10:46-52 (NKJV)
...As He went out of Jericho with His disciples and a great multitude, blind Bartimaeus, the son of Timaeus, sat by the road begging. And when he heard that it was Jesus of Nazareth, he began to cry out and say, "Jesus, Son of David, have mercy on me! Then many warned him to be quiet; but he cried out all the more...

In Jewish culture, illness and disability were believed to be a punishment from God for sin committed by the person or their parents. The crowd tries to silence Bartimaeus because in their opinion, he was not worthy to be heard by Jesus. The enemy of your soul will use the words of others to align with your deepest hurts, fears, regrets, and failures of your past, causing you to question and doubt. However, whatever they say has to align with God's Word. In those moments, God's voice needs to be the loudest!

1 Peter 5:8 (NKJV)
Be sober, be vigilant; because your adversary the devil walks about like a roaring lion, seeking whom he may devour.

The devil is not going to come out directly and say something that you know is a lie, but he will mix a painful chapter of your life together with his toxicity and present it as truth. He is aware of God's purposes for your life and is intent on stopping you dead in your tracks.

Any voice that says you need to lower your expectations or silences what God has put in your heart, is not a voice from God. Sometimes that voice can be your own. When the crowd around blind Bartimaeus tried to silence him, he shouted even louder (v48). When the voices around you are trying to silence God's voice you need to cry out even louder for God to reveal Himself to you. Jesus heard, stopped, and healed blind Bartimaeus. God hears you; He sees you; He will meet with you and reveal Himself to you.

February 21st – *Shimmering Saint*
Y1 – MATT 25 & 26 / Y2 - NEH 8 & 9

1 Corinthians 1:2 (NKJV)
... to those who are sanctified in Christ Jesus, called to be saints, with all who in every place call on the name of Jesus Christ our Lord, both theirs and ours.

A saint in the Bible doesn't refer to a pious or revered person, canonised by an ecclesiastical body. It refers to all who have been consecrated, set apart and declared Holy! That's you! You were a sinner... now you are a saint! A born again believer!

When you accepted Christ and turned from old habits, God wrenched you out of the miry clay where your feet were firmly entrenched, where your muddled mind was a mess, and then He put you in a place of stability. By a miracle you were no longer stuck.

Just like in a classroom, where the naughty children are asked to move to the back so they won't be a bad influence, God separated you. He wanted to make sure you were protected so that you wouldn't be hurt, damaged, or influenced by sin again. Sanctified and set apart by God's grace!

Ephesians 2:19 (NIV)
Consequently, you are no longer foreigners and strangers, but fellow citizens with God's people and also members of his household,

God is kind. He could see that need for separation long before you did. Before you were walking in darkness, but now shining in His glorious light because you have been redeemed by His blood. Born into a new life and family, graciously changed and blessed!

Father God, I thank You for finding me and putting me in a place of stability. Help me to appreciate all You have done for me and to remember that I am a new creation in You, no longer living a life of sin, but one that pleases You as a saint.

February 22nd – *Arising Mother*
Y1 - MATT 27 & 28 / Y2 - NEH 10 & 11

Judges 5:7 (NKJV)
Village life ceased, it ceased in Israel, until I, Deborah, arose, arose a mother in Israel.

When thinking about this, who better is there to give us a Godly example of rising to motherhood in our churches than Deborah?

Deborah rose to God's calling by leading Israel into battle. Barak didn't trust God enough to go into battle alone and asked her to come with him. She became like a mother to all Israel, caring about the children of God. She wasn't motivated by the achievements or title.[1] She wanted to fulfil the will of God and bring victory to the highland tribes. Whatever happened, she was going to be who Israel needed her to be. Spoiler alert - it was a great victory!

You will, if you have not already, have the privilege to serve people in your church who were either hurt by their mother or weren't raised with a mother at all. We come across mothers that do not respond to the needs of their children, put career or boyfriend ahead of their kids, or who have imparted hurt and brokenness because of sin. We as Pastor's wives are not here to take the role of a natural mother away, but we can, if someone extends the welcome, fill in the gap by embracing them as one of our own. We are to rise up to the needs of our congregation, to nurture, love, comfort, and guide.

Deborah 'arose a mother in Israel' and took on the responsibilities of the Israelite army.

Are you sensitive to the needs of your congregation? Would you describe yourself as a mother in God's church?

Ask God to equip you with all the resources you need to respond to the calling of a Pastor's wife and to be the mothering example sinners and saints need you to be.

February 23rd – *Historical Women*
Y1 – EX 1 & 2 / Y2 - NEH 12 & 13

Ann Hasseltine Judson

It was in the early hours of the morning when Adoniram (Ann's new husband) gently said, 'Ann, goodbyes are too painful, let's take the horse and carriage, grit our teeth, and begin the journey now whilst your family is asleep.' Ann agreed, but as they were quietly leaving the house, her father heard the hustle and ran downstairs, only to find that they had already gone. Devastated, he jumped on his horse, caught up and pleaded with them to return to say their official 'Goodbyes,' undoubtedly an emotional departure.

They boarded a ship to Burma, South East Asia on February 9th, 1812. It was a horrendous journey! The waves tossed and turned and as she lay on a lower deck and she started to experience contractions. After some time, she gave birth to a stillborn baby who was later buried at sea. After 18 months of travel, Adoniram carried his weak and mourning wife off the ship into the little town of Rangoon. The locals stared. The noise, language, destitution, filthy streets, overbearing heat, horrible smell, and naked children struck Ann to the very core. She said later, 'it was the unhappiest day of her life,' nevertheless, Ann overcame, adapted, and adopted the culture.

The people would say, 'Your religion is good for you, ours is for us.' For six years they contended with this response, the ears of the people were closed and none had accepted Jesus. Until one day, Maung Nau, a timber merchant attending the church, but unrepentant, stood up in a service and expressed his belief in Jesus and was baptised; an incredible breakthrough. Whilst Adoniram was preaching, studying, and translating the Bible into Burmese, Ann held meetings for women in her home. She showed them Jesus, but they had no interest. Finally, in June of 1820, because of Ann's witness, Mah Men-Lay was converted; the first female to confess Jesus and the tenth member of the church.

Isaiah 65:23 (NKJV)
They shall not labour in vain.

Ann died at the young age of 36, after experiencing many heart-breaking adversities, but she left behind a legacy. Ann was America's first female missionary and Burma's first Pastor's wife. When her husband died in 1850, he left behind 63 established Burmese churches and over 8,000 Burmese converts.

February 24th - *Testimony*

Y1 - PS 15 / Y2 - PS 119

My Pastor by Grace

During an altar call my Pastor said, 'Do not let pride stop you from speaking to your Pastor.'

Up until that point I had always avoided speaking to my Pastor. I knew I needed a Pastor, that God placed headship in our lives for a reason, and that submission to leadership can reflect our submission to God. But regardless of my respect for him, factors like feeling inadequate, pent up hurts, and fears contributed to my inability to communicate with him.

So, when I heard those words, the Spirit of God overwhelmed me and I found myself in bits; *'Was I too proud to speak to my own Pastor? Was pride hindering mental and spiritual freedom?'*

When the service was over, I immediately approached him. Weeping like a baby, I addressed issue after issue after issue with him, and to my surprise he listened, encouraged me, cared about me, and directed me. I left that conversation liberated; a weight having been lifted off. I felt like I could see clearly again.

I had believed a lie for so many years, 'You are just another person. He speaks highly of everyone but you.' I had even begun to believe that he thought my husband should have married someone else because I was useless. To this day that conversation with my Pastor is a milestone in my Christianity, a moment where God helped me to conquer my mind and pride. God ordains a Pastor for the sake of the people, a gift from God. Because of this change, I have been able to receive from his ministry more than I could ever imagine.

Hebrews 13:17 (NIV)
Have confidence in your leaders and submit to their authority because they keep watch over you...

Jeremiah 3:15 (NIV)
Then I will give you shepherds after my own heart, who will lead you with knowledge and understanding.

February 25th - *Study & Sermon notes*

Y1 - PS 16 / Y2 - PS 120

February 26th – *Doctor, Doctor*

Y1 - EX 3 & 4 / Y2 – TITUS 1 & 2

Mark 2:15-17 (NASB)
Many tax collectors and sinners were dining with Jesus...The scribes of the Pharisees...said to His disciples, 'Why is He eating and drinking with tax collectors and sinners?' And hearing this, Jesus said to them, 'It is not those who are healthy who need a physician, but those who are sick; I did not come to call the righteous, but sinners.'

The Gospel is medicine to a spiritually sick person. If you go to a doctor's surgery you will find sick people because that is why they go there. Jesus has medicine for the soul, therefore He goes where the spiritually sick people are because that is who needs Him.

The scribes and Pharisees had no understanding of this. In their minds, they were spiritually healthy and therefore stayed away from sinners. They had no concern for the hearts of people, but were only interested in the application of the law in society. As far as they were concerned, if you didn't practice the law you were good for nothing. They considered themselves righteous, and because they kept the law, felt no need for Jesus the Saviour.

They were offended and outraged to find Jesus fellowshipping with sinners, 'Why is He eating and drinking with tax collectors and sinners?' In their mind, the 'true Messiah' would not eat with sinners. Jesus tackles their twisted mindsets head on. He boldly declares that He has come for the sake of these unrighteous people because their souls need fixing. He exposed the self-righteousness that caused these religious leaders to look down their noses at sinners.

Romans 3:10 (NKJV)
As it is written there is no one righteous, no not one.

Jesus loves sinners, despite their sin. Society shames them, but Jesus was not ashamed. He travelled with them, ate with them, and even stayed in their homes. He embraced them and showed them how to live a life that was pleasing to God and we are to do exactly the same.

February 27th – *The Encourager*

Y1 - EX 5 & 6 / Y2 – TITUS 3

1 Samuel 30:6 (KJV)
...but David encouraged himself in the Lord his God.

Isn't it funny how in the midst of the ebbs and flows of life, one word of encouragement can brighten your day and put a spring back in your step?

'To encourage' is the action of giving someone support, confidence, or hope.

There was one particular character in the bible, Joses, who was known for his ability to encourage people by instilling confidence in them. This gift was so profound that the apostles gave him the nickname Barnabas, which means 'son of encouragement' (Acts 4:36). They probably called him 'Barnie the encourager'! However, our text isn't about skilfully encouraging others, but it relates to you and the need to encourage yourself. David had lots of problems in life, many of them caused by himself, but he was able to encourage himself in God, and in doing so had a tremendous ability to move on in life. This is probably one of the reasons why God called David 'a man after his own heart' (1 Samuel 13:14).

What if each pastor's wife got paid for every set back, she experienced? She would be a millionaire! *But how rich would she be if she got paid for every time, she strengthened herself in the Lord, got back up and continued?* We have a need for encouragement on a daily basis, but who and where can it come from? The answer is simple, YOU! In a moment of struggle, offense, or let down, learn to keep perspective, and move past it. Remember to 'pick your battles' and not allow yourself to get caught up in every problem as it only bogs you down. Speak words of hope over your own life and you will surely have the victory. Practice encouraging others by encouraging yourself.

Psalm 42:11 (NKJV)
Why are you cast down, O my soul? And why are you disquieted within me? Hope in God; For I shall yet praise Him, The help of my countenance and my God.

February 28th –*Royal Crown*
Y1 - EX 7 & 8 / Y2 – ESTH 1 & 2

Esther 1:12 (NKJV)
But Queen Vashti refused to come at the king's command...

King Ahasuerus is on the throne and is having a massive party. It's the seventh day and he is getting a little merry. He has this great idea and demands that his wife (Vashti) parades around the banquet in her royal crown as 'she was beautiful to behold.' Some commentators say that the whole idea of this exploitation came from an argument the men were having about which country had the most beautiful women. Regardless, Vashti refused to be objectified, disobeyed his command, and was consequently stripped of her title and banished.

Because of her strong moral principles, Vashti lost everything. She was a woman of integrity.

Would you do the same if you were in her situation?

Your immediate response would be in the affirmative, but if you weigh up the loss, you might think again. Vashti wasn't a Christian woman, she served other gods, but when faced with this choice she put righteousness above relationship. She had sound judgment, was undivided in her opinions, and recognised right from wrong.

Pastor's wives can often find themselves in compromising situations. Maybe a lady in church is 'offloading' on you, but you can discern that she is 'digging for information' and sowing seeds of disunity. *Do you shut down the conversation or condone what she is saying by politely listening?*

We have an obligation to emulate Christ and sometimes there is a cost. Shutting down an ungodly conversation may be awkward and cause people to dislike you, but it is essential for the sake of the other person's salvation. Our example is critical because people always reference our conduct. If Vashti agreed to 'parade herself' it would have not only led the men at the banquet to sin, but it would have given an air of acceptability for this behaviour to the women of the nation. Ask God to help you navigate the Christian life with integrity and to obtain the skill of winning people through it.

Time to purchase your next Devotional book

Volume 2

April – May – June

March 1st – *Missionaries Wife*

Y1 – EX 9 & 10 / Y2 – ESTH 3 & 4

Matthew 19:29 (NLT)
And everyone who has given up houses or brothers or sisters or father or mother or children or property, for my sake, will receive a hundred times as much in return and will inherit eternal life.

Adam Clarke's commentary says, 'A glorious portion for a persevering believer! The fullness of Grace here, and the fullness of Glory hereafter!' [1] This ministers to every heart but particularly that of the missionary's wife. There is nothing as dear to our hearts than God's Word as it's relevant in all seasons.

A HEARTFELT CRY
The new day has dawned,
My heart is being torn.
A part of me is missing,
It lies over the seas, distancing!
Precious are my children, comes the cry from my heart,
For we are far apart.
My children will never know the ache and despair
at not being there in their darkest hour;
But I know there is someone else there in love and power,
His name is Jesus!
My God sees us;
He is here with me, a part of me, holding me, hearing me,
Seeing me on my knees for my family.
The tears flow, the prayers going out!
Let's give a victory shout;
Oh how I know the heart of the missionary's wife,
Oh my God visit her as she's paying the price,
Hold her close! To her heart gently speak
Giving her hope and peace
Knowing Lord it won't be long
When this life is over, we'll all be gone.
Into Your Kingdom we will go, praising you evermore!
Soon You will open the door
And we will be with You for all eternity.
Thank You Lord for watching over my family,
For Your word is faithful and true
To the promises You made to those who serve You!

By Coral Perry

March 2nd – *Abigail's Qualities*
Y1 – EX 11 & 12 / Y2 – ESTH 5 & 6

I Samuel 25:23-24 (NKJV)
Now when Abigail saw David, she dismounted quickly from the donkey, fell on her face before David, and bowed down to the ground. So, she fell at his feet and said: "On me, my lord, on me let this iniquity be! And please let your maidservant speak in your ears and hear the words of your maidservant.

Prior to this scripture, David sent men to ask for supplies from Nabal who refused. David told his men to gird up and go to attack Nabal, but one of Nabal's men told Abigail. She gathered food and supplies for David and his men and went to meet them, but she didn't tell Nabal. Abigail apologises to David for the wrongdoing, which he accepts and tells her to go in peace. Within Abigail's apology, she asks for forgiveness and also turns David's eyes to the Lord.

I Samuel 25:28 (NKJV)
Please forgive the trespass of your maidservant. For the LORD will certainly make for my lord an enduring house, because my lord fights the battles of the LORD, and evil is not found in you throughout your days.

Abigail is quick and shows herself to be humble, apologising on behalf of her husband and saving her entire household from attack. It diffused the emotion and changed David's course of action. There may be situations we are in within our marriage, other relationships, or in the church where an apology could bring change and make a difference. We must be humble and sensitive to our surroundings. This does not mean we need to apologise to all people for someone else's wrongdoings, but it shows the humility and trust in God we need.

Lord, forgive me that I have allowed my pride to prevent me from apologising. Help me in the future to humble myself, to apologise and change the situation. Give me words to speak when apologising that are full of wisdom, guiding people to You.

March 3rd - *Testimony*

Y1 – PS 17 / Y2 – PS 121

Natasha's Salvation Story (PT. 1)

I grew up in a Christian family, going to church every Sunday, but I didn't really understand much or listen to the sermons, I just wanted to be with my friends. When my teenage years hit, I became rebellious and decided that I wouldn't go to church anymore.

Throughout my school years I was bullied for the way I looked, dressed, and for what I had (and didn't have). So when I was old enough to get a job and earn my own money, I spent it on fake nails, hair extensions, eye lashes, fake tan, and the latest clothes in order to change my appearance to fit in and be liked.

Then I found social media, and with my new 'fake' look I quickly realized that it attracted guys, something I had never experienced before. I ended up meeting a man online who I talked with, day and night, for 3 years. I pushed my whole family away because they told me he was no good for me and basically became a hermit. We hadn't even met in person, yet I had 'fallen in love' with him, and pulled in by his charms and good looks, I did things I never thought I would do. This guy had full control over me, what I did, who I spoke to, everything. In time I started to comprehend that something wasn't right and tried to leave him, but I just could not get away. The mental abuse was unbearable and there were times he would threaten to kill himself if I broke up with him. His family had kicked him out and drug dealers were after him; I felt there was nothing I could do, I was all he had! The mind games and control really messed with me.

In addition to this, I was regularly bullied by a girl in my 6th form. One day, utterly broken, I left the school grounds and sat by the edge of the road on a corner. I was ready to end this misery, but when I stepped out onto the road, I noticed that it was my mum's car! I fell to my knees crying. I wish I could say this was the end of it, but it was just the beginning. I did finally get away from this guy, but I was still searching for something to fill the void.

To be continued...

March 4th - *Study & Sermon notes*

Y1 – PS 18 / Y2 – PS 122

March 5ᵗʰ – *Mighty El-Shaddai*
Y1 – EX 13 & 14 / Y2 – ESTH 7 & 8

Jeremiah 32:27 (NIV)
I am the Lord, the God of all mankind. Is anything too hard for me?

God Almighty is the most common meaning given to God's name 'El-Shaddai,' however, *do you understand the weight that this name carries?* Whilst this may seem simple on the surface, 'El-Shaddai' goes deeper and means so much more.

'El' is translated as God, Mighty, Power, Strong, and could by itself be interpreted as 'God Almighty.' So, what does 'Shaddai' mean? 'Shaddai' is formed from the Hebrew word 'shad' which derives from the word for breast. It signifies the strength giver, the nourisher, the one who pours himself into others. It means that God is all sufficient, and life finds its source in Him. Whilst the scripture I've chosen in Jeremiah doesn't expressly mention El-Shaddai, it perfectly describes what His name means! [1]

Not only does El-Shaddai means that God is almighty and all-sufficient. It also means He is the giver of fruitfulness. El-Shaddai is first found in **Genesis 17:1-2 (ESV), When Abram was ninety-nine years old the LORD appeared to Abram and said to him, 'I am God Almighty; walk before me, and be blameless, that I may make my covenant between me and you, and may multiply you greatly.'** God promised to make Abram fruitful, which at the time was impossible for Abram! He needed a miracle, and only an Almighty God who is the source of all life could do this; and He did! Abraham became the father of nations. **Genesis 17:5 (ESV) ... for I have made you the father of a multitude of nations.**[2]

How incredible that we are invited, even hand selected, to dine with the King! This Almighty, all-sufficient, giver of nations wants a personal and intimate relationship with us! He is our source of strength and fruitfulness.

March 6th – *Be Acknowledged*
Y1 – EX 15 & 16 / Y2 – ESTH 9 & 10

Revelation 3:5 (NIV)
The one who is victorious will, like them, be dressed in white. I will never blot out the name of that person from the book of life, but will acknowledge that name before my Father and his angels.

(NLT)
All who are victorious will be clothed in white. I will never erase their names from the Book of Life, but I will announce before my Father and his angels that they are mine.

As Christians, we can never forget that a day is coming when we will stand before God and it will be decided where we spend the rest of eternity. Thank God that through His wonderful grace and mercy we know what that decision will be.

No matter how hard your life is, the craziness going on in the world, and the unrighteousness that seems to prevail, do not forget this is not our forever home. For the day is coming when our physical bodies will be left behind, the sins of this world will no longer affect us, and we will be with God forevermore. The true life is yet to come. Even as Christians, we will face a judgement, but if we are victorious in standing for righteousness, we will be dressed in white. Praise God! We can be encouraged that the best is yet to come.

We need to be diligent to prioritise our relationship with Jesus as the most precious thing. It's not about our acts of service, how many people are in our church, nor how many songs we write, only through a relationship with Jesus will He acknowledge us as His. It will be a higher honour to have our name in that Book of Life than in any book of recognition for the world's finest princes, poets, statesman or nobles. So be encouraged, the best is yet to come!

March 7th – *Poorest Preacher*

Y1 – EX 17 & 18 / Y2 – PHILEMON 1

1 Corinthians 9:8-12 (NKJV)
Do I say these things as a *mere* man? Or does not the law say the same also? For it is written in the law of Moses, "You shall not muzzle an ox while it treads out the grain." Is it oxen God is concerned about? Or does He say *it* altogether for our sakes? For our sakes, no doubt, *this* is written, that he who plows should plow in hope, and he who threshes in hope should be partaker of his hope. If we have sown spiritual things for you, *is it* a great thing if we reap your material things? If others are partakers of *this* right over you, *are* we not even more?"

After one Sunday worship service, a little boy told the pastor, 'When I grow up, I'm going to give you some money.' 'Well, thank you,' the pastor replied, 'but why?' The boy said, 'Because my daddy says you're one of the poorest preachers we've ever had.'

The need for finances within the church is great and often at times stretched thin. Like a business, the church resources fund the running of the building, local events, equipment, and lastly pays the pastor a wage.

1 Timothy 5:18
A labourer is worthy of his wages.

Every ministering couple goes through quiet seasons, but for the most part they work flat out serving the needs of their congregation and evangelising in their city. They function in different roles, but work as a team. Many couples work a secular job alongside running a church to cover the cost of their living expenses- this is tough. The call to ministry requires personal sacrifice, but there should come a time of growth when we receive a decent, consistent wage. The state of the ministry directly impacts our family and where we see a need, it is our responsibility to contend for it. God *can* and *will* bring an abundance.

In **Exodus 34:4-5**, the Israelites are rebuilding the tabernacle and the bible records the people bringing so many offerings that Moses had to tell them to stop. Imagine that! Amen!

March 8th – *Program Princess*
Y1 – EX 19 & 20 / Y2 – JOB 1 & 2

John 3:5-6 (NKJV)
Jesus answered, "Most assuredly, I say to you, unless one is born of water and the Spirit, he cannot enter the kingdom of God. That which is born of the flesh is flesh, and that which is born of the Spirit is spirit."

Nicodemus was a member of the Jewish council and as a Pharisee was heavily involved in Jewish rituals.[1] However, despite social influence, he desired to know the living God, rather than the God of the law. Jesus tells him that it is not the flesh that makes us right with God but the Spirit. By being born again we can come to know the Father.

Galatians 2:21 (NLT)
For if keeping the law could make us right with God, then there was no need for Christ to die.

As Pastor's wives we are involved in many things. Several services, bible studies, prayer meetings, and so much more. It's easy to hide behind tasks and neglect the real reason behind these activities, which is a personal relationship and a desire to serve in God's Kingdom. We can associate the word religion with rules, programmes, and systems. If we are not careful, we can lose the desire that Nicodemus displays and become busy church workers without a real relationship with Jesus...just like the Pharisees.

Lord help me not to become so consumed by tasks that I forget to serve You in the right way. Keep my heart focused on being used in the kingdom out of love and not just obedience. I am born again in the Spirit by Your Son Jesus Christ, thank You for making this simple. Help me to not over complicate things with rituals so that I would miss out on the plans and destiny that You have for my life. Amen.

March 9th – *Todays Footmen*
Y1 – EX 21 & 22 / Y2 – JOB 3 & 4

Jeremiah 12:5 (NIV)
If you have raced with men on foot and they have worn you out, how can you compete with horses? If you stumble in safe country, how will you manage in the thickets by the Jordan?

Prior to this verse, Jeremiah is 'having it out' with God, questioning and giving Him a piece of his mind if you will. He is grieved with the persecution he has been suffering and asks God, 'Why are the wicked prospering?' To which God replies, (my paraphrase), 'Are you kidding me? You are living in your own country, safe and sound, yet you are exhausted by the problems you face with your peers. You know I have much greater plans in store for you, but before you progress to fighting the men on horseback, you must first handle the men on foot. Your mind is so far ahead that you neglect working on the character building issues of *today*.'

If men find themselves unable to contend with a less power, it is in vain for them to fight against a greater power. The Lord is advising us, just as He did Jeremiah, to focus on the issues of today. Obsessing over future matters is a waste of your time if you can't process the smaller, more current issues. These are the lessons that prepare and equip you for the future in the first place.

Matthew 6:34 (NIV)
Therefore, do not worry about tomorrow, for tomorrow will worry about itself. Each day has enough trouble of its own.

Be uplifted. Today's victory over the footmen is the qualification for tomorrow's victory amongst the horsemen.

March 10th - *Testimony*

Y1 – PS 19 / Y2 – PS 123

Continued...

Natasha's Salvation Story (PT. 2)

I found a new set of friends who drank, slept around, and took drugs so I embraced this lifestyle for a few years. I started dating a guy I went to school with and my life changed forever when I found out I was pregnant! He wanted nothing to do with me or 'it' (our baby) and when I told him and he became abusive, demanding that I have an abortion. With that in mind, I left him.

In March 2013, my brother asked me to come to a church service. I wasn't sure what the pastor was talking about, but by the end, I knew I needed to respond. That night I accepted Jesus Christ and instantly felt a weight lifted. The lady who prayed with me invited me to breakfast the following Wednesday. We clicked and I remember telling her, 'I'm pregnant, but I'm planning on getting an abortion!' She looked shocked but gently said, 'Don't get an abortion, that will upset God.' She helped me understand God's plan for myself and my unborn child.

Still confused, I kept an appointment at an abortion clinic. My new friend from church came and sat in the lobby, telling me later that she was continually praying for me to have the strength to do the right thing. By the grace of God, I kept my beautiful baby boy. At this point my life really started to change. I fully gave myself to Jesus and was filled with such joy that I wanted to share it with others. I attended every church service, outreach, concert, and fellowship. I was so happy and content with Jesus, I felt I didn't need anything else, but God had different plans. Eight months after having my son I started dating a wonderful man and yes, we got married. He not only took me as his wife, but lovingly adopted my son and became his father.

Romans 5:8 (NKJV)
For God demonstrates his love towards us in that whilst we were still sinners Christ died for us.

I thank God every day for all He has done for me. We don't deserve anything, but God loves us so much that He gave His son so that we could be saved.

March 11th - *Study & Sermon notes*

Y1 – PS 20 / Y2 – PS 124

March 12th – *Despite Persecution*
Y1 – EX 23 & 24 / Y2 – JOB 5 & 6

Hebrews 11:23 (NIV)
By faith Moses' parents hid him for three months after he was born, because they saw he was no ordinary child, and they were not afraid of the king's edict.

Moses was born when the Israelites were slaves in Egypt. His mother Jochebed was well aware of Pharaoh's order to kill all newborn sons because of Egyptian fear that Israel was becoming too strong, yet she decided in faith to keep her child; a crime punishable by death. Realising she could not hide a crying baby from the Egyptian guards forever while protecting two other children, she created a basket with tar and pitch, safely strapped baby Moses inside, and placed it on the bank of the River Nile. She trusted that God would somehow bring salvation to her son and indeed He did. Moses ended up in the hands of the Queen, and by a miracle Jochebed became employed as his nursemaid. In a time of national persecution, God did a miracle and gave protection and provision for their needs.

You are a child of God and have access to the full realm of God's provision and power. Yes, we live in a world where there may be times of persecution and great need but, never forget that we serve an all knowing God who works behind the scenes. We can praise God, regardless of what we are seeing or experiencing because we know He is winning the victory in the spiritual dimension. We do not always comprehend the dominion we have been given or how God is moving for His glory, but we can trust He is at work! Cry out to the Lord to move in the miracle realm for provision in your situation and keep your eyes on things above.

Father, I know that during persecution you are with me, but I am asking you to give me the strength and authority to rise above it. Give me a revelation and vision to carry me through. In Jesus name. Amen.

March 13th – *Praying Ancestors*

Y1 – EX 25 & 26 / Y2 – JOB 7 & 8

Daniel 2:19-20,23 (NLT)
That night the secret was revealed to Daniel in a vision. Then Daniel praised the God of heaven, saying..."I thank and praise the God of my ancestors, for You have given me wisdom and strength. You have told me what we asked of You and revealed to us what the king demanded."

Daniel praising the God of his 'ancestors' shows me how crucial it is for me to help my children cultivate their relationship with God at a young age. Anything Godly or righteous that we put into our children is never wasted, pointless, or unproductive. Our example can equip them to have a dynamic relationship with God. Let it be from us that they learn to call upon Him in all situations, praising God in all circumstances, both good and bad.

The salvation of my children has been at times the cause of great concern. Whilst there have been no easy answers or explanations in the midst of that distress, one of the things that I hold on to is that I have tried my best to be obedient to God by raising them in His ways and not mine. This scripture gives me hope that there is a place in each child's heart, irrespective of age, where they can cry out to God and He will hear them.

Why not do some digging into your ancestry? Could it be that there was a bible believing, Spirit filled, great, great grandfather somewhere along the line praying for you? *Why not cover your future generations in prayer?* God sees your heart, hears your prayers, and He honours the requests of the saints.

Father, I ask that You equip me to teach my children to have the relationship with You that You desire. Let me be reliant on the Holy Spirit and teach them with love and joy. Let me realise that anything I do is in Your strength and not mine. Amen.

March 14th – *Proverbs 31:1-5*

Y1 – EX 27 & 28 / Y2 – JOB 9 & 10

Proverbs 31:1-2 (ESV)
The words of King Lemuel. An oracle that his mother taught him: What are you doing, my son? What are you doing, son of my womb? What are you doing, son of my vows?

Can you hear the anguish in her voice? Is she wagging her finger or pleading?

Proverbs 31:3-5 (ESV)
Do not give your strength to women, your ways to those who destroy kings. It is not for kings, O Lemuel, it is not for kings to drink wine, or for rulers to take strong drink, lest they drink and forget what has been decreed and pervert the rights of all the afflicted.

Wine in those days was common, and most often the bible referred simply to crushed grapes. The grapes were reduced to a syrup and they would add one part of this syrup to two parts of water. It was basically grape juice. However, after fermentation wine could become incredibly intoxicating.

Mum is saying, 'Son, you cannot afford to make a fool out of yourself.' Fully aware of previous examples of kings, she knew that leadership could go to the head. It's a warning to her son that when you drink the strong stuff it loosens convictions, reason, judgement, and it perverts the heart. She is simply making the point that he is not like the other children but set apart and chosen. We too have been set apart and chosen by God for His purposes. We live in a world full of lapsed standards, but God's standards never change. This mother has put her mind to the task of preparing her son for his future and has unreservedly invested in him. Do you do the same?

Lord Jesus, I am grateful that You have given me influence over my children and others around me. Help me to communicate effectively, whether it be in action or speech, about You and how to live a God glorifying life. Help me to bring warning confidently, yet sensitively to those who are going astray, trusting that You will use me to draw them back to You. Amen.

March 15th – *Proverbs 31:6-11*

Y1 – EX 29 & 30 / Y2 – JOB 11 & 12

Proverbs 31:6-9 (KJV)
Let beer be for those who are perishing, wine for those who are in anguish! Let him drink, and forget his poverty, and remember his misery no more. Open thy mouth for the dumb in the cause of all such as are appointed to destruction. Open thy mouth, judge righteously, and plead the cause of the poor and needy.

This advice is spoken from the heart of a mother to ensure that her son is not derailed from his destiny. King Lemuel's mother reiterates verses 3- 5 that wine is good as relief to the dying but is of no value to those with purpose and responsibility. She then states that with his position comes the potential to use authority in assisting those in need. We too have been given a position through our role, not to judge, but to ensure that the most vulnerable are treated well and not exploited.

Proverbs 31:10-11 (KJV)
Who can find a virtuous woman? for her price is far above rubies. The heart of her husband doth safely trust in her, so that he shall have no need of spoil.

The beginning of this verse is the most cherished guidance for wives around the world and has been held in high esteem and memorised throughout history. Its truth is timeless. When we conduct ourselves biblically, we have a worth beyond rubies! *Can he safely trust in you?* This awareness should also extend to how we view and treat family and church resources. *Do we carefully consider the impact of our behaviour upon that which he works so hard for?* We all strive for a trusting relationship in marriage, but the bible helps us see that trust is dependent upon our actions.

God, we thank You for Your word. Help us to use this to guide and consider how we carry ourselves. Let us comprehend how our conduct impacts not just our destiny, but also our marriage and ministry.

March 16th – *Proverbs 31:12-16*

Y1 – EX 31 & 32 / Y2 – JOB 13 & 14

Proverbs 31:12 (NKJV)
She does him good and not evil all the days of her life.

A virtuous wife is decent and never wicked, and she continues being a blessing. She is reliable and not fickle.[1] *Do you consider the impact of your actions towards your husband?*

Proverbs 31:13-16 (NKJV)
She seeks wool and flax, and willingly works with her hands. She is like the merchant ships, she brings her food from afar. She also rises while it is yet night, and provides food for her household, And a portion for her maidservants. She considers a field and buys it; From her profits she plants a vineyard.

She looks for useful materials: The wife is intuitive and knows how to find resources for her household. Even travels long distances to find food; out of her way and being inconvenienced.

She works with her hands. She is not proud or condescending and does not think that working with her hands is beneath her.[1] What is noteworthy is that she works *willingly*; there is not a spirit of resentment behind the work. It is a pleasure for her. She, at the expense of needed sleep, is prepared to rise early before others in order to be organised.

She considers business opportunities. She is thoughtful and invests financially when a potential profit could be made and with it, she invests again. This requires hard work but ensures long term safety for her family's future. 1

These verses show that our day to day tasks (which often we consider to be normal, mundane housework) are highly valued by God. Let's face it, we may not need to buy a field and plant a vineyard (thank goodness), but there are certainly other innovative ideas we can develop to bless our families. Lord help us!

March 17th - *Testimony*

Y1 – PS 21 / Y2 – PS 125

Black Dog by Melissa

I was raised by two parents, wonderful, but unsaved. Both had been completely broken by the abuse, neglect, and rejections of the past and serious devastating depression was in full flow in their lives. My mother raised me to hate men because of all she experienced, but no matter how hard I tried, I radiated vulnerability resulting in many helpless situations under the hands of men stronger than me. At school, I was bullied and this destroyed my confidence and contributed to a foundation in my heart for extreme self-hatred. One day (almost thirty years ago) thanks be to God, my father committed his heart to Jesus and we witnessed a noticeable transformation. It was this miracle that led my mother and I to salvation.

Fast forward a few years, I met and married an amazing man in our church. He felt called to preach so I followed him to three different cities. I loved my husband and wanted to obey God. I didn't realise, however, that my own suppressed problem with depression could manifest. Naturally, I am not a people person, and though I've softened over the years, trust issues (established as a child) and the need to protect myself continued years into my Christianity.

Because of this, I felt completely uncomfortable serving or being in large gatherings. Every year my husband and I would book to attend seminars and bible conferences, so we could be fed, challenged, and rebooted, but these gatherings posed the greatest conflict for me. Of course, I wanted to be there, but the anxiety was through the roof, I just couldn't face it. Why? I battled with the same tendencies as my father; my mind couldn't see light and I was filled with self-hate. I would ask myself, 'How can a Christian be depressed?' I sought Godly counsel, prayed, changed my diet, but it resulted only in slight improvement and not deliverance. I lived like this for 23 years! Why me? Why now?

On our last mission, our family experienced continuous and some profoundly serious assaults from the enemy, which led to our returning home. We needed respite. Whilst my journey has been painful and at times unbearable, I believe that God used all this to peel back the layers of my life, expose them, and ultimately bring healing. Without it, I sometimes question whether I would have been able to overcome that debilitating mental sickness. Over time I have experienced deliverance, my mind is more stable than ever, and my heart has healed. Only now can I accept being loved.

Have you ever felt low, incredibly low? Have you ever felt like you're being consumed by darkness? You see your children, have a conversation with your husband, attend a Holy Spirit filled church service, yet your mind is numb, life is foggy, and vision is impaired. Please heed my words, you must acknowledge depression and understand that it is not your portion, nor is it from God, but a strategy from hell. Take authority, stand on the truth and Jesus *will* put a song in your heart.

Psalms 40:1-3 (ESV)
I waited patiently for the LORD; he inclined to me and heard my cry. He drew me up from the pit of destruction, out of the miry bog, and set my feet upon a rock, making my steps secure. He put a new song in my mouth, a song of praise to our God. Many will see and fear and put their trust in the LORD.

March 18th - *Study & Sermon notes*

Y1 – PS 22 / Y2 – PS 126

March 19th – *Proverbs 31:17-21*

Y1 – EX 33 & 34 / Y2 – JOB 15 & 16

Proverbs 31: 17-21 (NKJV)

This section of proverbs discusses strength and compassion.

17 She girds herself with strength...
The virtuous wife is noted for her strength, and it is strength in action (her arms). When you 'gird' yourself it is in preparation for some kind of heroic or difficult task. One example I've heard is 'like hard running,' but I prefer the example of 'keeping one or more small children alive each day!'

18 She perceives that her merchandise is good, and her lamp does not go out by night ...
A wise woman knows what to buy and she knows quality (don't worry you can learn this)! She works hard to take care of things, and the light stays on until the job is done.

19 She stretches out her hands to the distaff, and her hand holds the spindle.
A distaff was a short staff that held a bundle of fibres like flax or wool, ready to be spun into yarn or thread. In bible times, even if you were a wealthy woman you didn't think manual work was beneath you. 'Whatever you do, work heartily, as for the Lord...' (Colossians 3:23 ESV). The virtuous woman of Proverbs 31 worked hard in all that she put her hands to.

20 She extends her hand to the poor, yes, she reaches out her hands to the needy.
This verse speaks directly of her compassion. Although she could be perceived as well off, she is not proud and doesn't seek her wealth only for herself and her family but, cares for the poor and shows practical love.

21 She is not afraid of snow for her household, for all her household is clothed with scarlet.
A virtuous wife is so sure of God's provision that she ceases to worry when hard times hit; she can see past the current situation and know that God is faithful and always comes through.

March 20th – *Proverbs 31:22-26*

Y1 – EX 35 & 36 / Y2 – JOB 17 & 18

Proverbs 31:22-26 (NKJV)

22-24 She makes tapestry for herself; Her clothing is fine linen and purple. Her husband is known in the gates, when he sits among the elders of the land. She makes linen garments and sells them and supplies sashes for the merchants.

Purple was very highly esteemed and is the colour suitable for royalty and those of authority. Although we are not queens, could the scripture be talking about dressing appropriately for our stations or position, whether at church, home, or out with friends and family. Whatever the occasion, make sure your dress glorifies God and not the world.

25 Strength and honour are her clothing; She shall rejoice in time to come.
Strength is a strong theme in this chapter (Vs 17 & 25) Her strength is lauded, not of body, but of mind and heart. She has the confidence to laugh without fear of the future, wearing it like a garment, fully trusting in God for His protection and provision.

26 She opens her mouth with wisdom, and on her tongue is the law of kindness.
When she opens her mouth, (for it is not always open) she expresses herself in a discreet and prudent manner; as well as, speaking of things not foolish and trifling, but of the moment and importance, and of usefulness to others: or 'concerning wisdom.' Take a moment to think about your own actions and the things you allow to fly off the tongue. Teach kindness by using words of grace, mercy, and righteousness.

Lord help me to take each of these scriptures and apply them to my life. Guard my heart from the world's perspective of virtue and forge me to become who You want me to be. Lord help me to withhold my tongue and speak words of kindness and grace. Amen.

March 21st – *Proverbs 31:27-31*

Y1 – EX 37 & 38 / Y2 – JOB 19 & 20

Proverbs 31: 27 (NLT)
She carefully watches everything in her household and suffers nothing from laziness.

To 'carefully watch' means to provide or seriously consider, in this case, the family's household.
We make sure that our children are attended to by communicating, teaching, and correcting them. Our husbands need someone to talk to, listen, and sit down and relax with. Our chores include working on the house, preparing the beds, cooking, and laundry; all somewhat tiring, but incredibly important and rewarding (when done with the right heart).

28-29 Her children stand and bless her. Her husband praises her: "There are many virtuous and capable women in the world, but you surpass them all!"
How wonderful. Praise from other people is one thing but being praised by your husband and children makes the effort we put in worth it! One compliment goes a long way, the sense of appreciation and value is priceless. *Who can you compliment today?*

30-31 Charm is deceptive, and beauty does not last; but a woman who fears the Lord will be greatly praised. Reward her for all she has done. Let her deeds publicly declare her praise.
Our world values the outward appearance and individuals are consumed with constant improvement. If you look good you qualify, which as we know can be deceptive. It seems conversation about developing character and the internal matters of the heart are at an all time low. The woman in this text has a healthy, reverent fear of the Lord and understands that her bingo wings, wrinkles, and bags under her eyes aren't going to impact people as much as what flows out of her heart and mouth.

How often do you judge a book by its cover? In other words, how often do you make assumptions of someone based on appearance, only to find when you get to know them, they are quite the opposite and your judgment? External beauty naturally fades with time, but a Godly character when nurtured will continually flourish and will be a source of praise.

March 22nd – *Perfected Faith*
Y1 – EX 39 & 40 / Y2 – JOB 21 & 22

James 2:22-26 (NKJV)
Do you see that faith was working together with his works, and by works faith was made perfect? And the Scripture was fulfilled which says, "Abraham believed God, and it was accounted to him for righteousness." And he was called the friend of God. You see then that a man is justified by works, and not by faith only. Likewise, was not Rahab the harlot also justified by works when she received the messengers and sent them out another way? For as the body without the spirit is dead, so faith without works is dead also".

Our genuine faith in God will lead to obedience and good works as this scripture says. If Abraham hadn't believed God, he would not have obeyed when God asked him to sacrifice his son. His faith in God was proven to be true because he obeyed.[1]

Rahab also proved her faith to be living because she believed, took the Israelite spies in, hid them, and helped them escape. Her faith in God wouldn't have saved her if she had not obeyed, and the city would have been destroyed with Rahab still inside.

James says their faith is demonstrated, perfected, and completed through their works. Matthew Henry's commentary says, 'Faith is the root and good works the fruits and we must have both.'[2]

Does your faith cause you to act? Is it living? What is God asking you to do?

Lord, let my faith be living and lead to obedience; that my good works will prove and perfect my faith. That I would trust You in all You ask of me and help me in my unbelief. Amen.

March 23rd – *Picture Perfect*

Y1 – ACT 1 & 2 / Y2 – JOB 23 & 24

1 Peter 4:9 (NKJV)
Be hospitable to one another without grumbling.

I was stressed, overworked, and exhausted, but every job in the house was completed for when our guest arrived. After shouting at my child and being frustrated with my husband, the thought occurred, 'Was it all worth it?' I broke down in tears. I had tried so hard to make everything perfect, caused myself and my family so much unnecessary stress, all for a guest who was just happy to be there.

Peter tells us to be hospitable without murmuring or complaining. This insinuates that there will always be something to grumble about (the house is too small or the kids are too noisy). Hospitality is not always easy or convenient, but it is essential. It blesses others, it shows our obedience to God, and demonstrates an example to our church (It is also a source of great joy). *How can we expect others to open their homes if we don't teach them?*

Luke 7:44 (NLV) He turned to the woman and said to Simon, "Do you see this woman? I came into your house and you gave Me no water to wash My feet. She washed My feet with her tears and dried them with the hairs of her head.

Jesus practiced hospitality without a home and generosity without a salary.[1] Jesus took in those who were imperfect, and he stayed in imperfect places.

Perfectionism is a pride or fear-based compulsion that either fuels our obsessive fixation on doing something perfectly or paralyzes us from acting at all; both of which often result in the harmful neglect of other necessary or good things.[2] It's good for things to be clean and tidy, but don't let it hinder the joy that someone could experience from a simple meal with their Pastor and his family. Let's place our eyes on those that need encouragement, friendship, and wisdom at an imperfectly perfect dinner table.

Remember, life is about people.

March 24ᵗʰ – *Testimony*

Y1 – PS 23 / Y2 – PS 127

Household Salvation by Jacqui

I was saved whilst abroad, in an age with no mobile phones or internet, so I wrote letters to my parents and friends telling them about Jesus. I phoned them excited one night recounting that, 'I flew through the air to the altar to repent, God touched me and now I'm changed.' My mum was organising to send someone to kidnap me! My brother actually got into a fight over his 'crazy sister.' When I returned home, I stayed only two weeks, then moved to a different city to be closer to church. My parents felt the shame of their golden daughter abandoning all they had raised her to believe and they had to live through the reproach and questioning from their community.

However, God covers our mistakes, and through time as I matured, I realised that my love for Jesus needed to be <u>demonstrated</u> to my family and friends, sometimes the hardest people to reach. I needed the power of prayer and listening to the Holy Ghost for wisdom to love them.

I got a call at work on a Friday from my brother, 'Mum had a mild heart attack early this morning, she is having a stent inserted, no need to fly up, she will be fine.' I decided that I would go visit in a few weeks as work was very busy. The next day I had planned to go to Heathrow to collect friends from America who had a day layover on their way to a medical mission. I felt the Holy Ghost prompt me early that morning to pack a small suitcase. One of the ladies was a very experienced cardiac nurse and she asked if she could speak to the consultant. 'Wow, ok.' After the call she clarified that mum had a massive heart attack and she was not confident with the drug treatment prescribed; most importantly, I needed to fly up and be with her. We prayed together, I booked a flight, dropped them back at the airport and flew home. The next day the consultant confirmed mum was going to die. I boldly spoke to her, she accepted Christ into her life and with an incredible peace and bravery, she said her goodbyes to everyone in the next two days. I stayed with her through that time, praying with her, massaging her body, and loving her into eternity.

Through that experience, my sister-in-law, my brother, and nephew became Christians. Amen!

Three years later, my dad was diagnosed with bone cancer, so he went to live with my brother. We had two years, spending time with him, reminiscing, getting to know him in a different way, and then one night he asked my brother to pray for his salvation. A month later, I spent a week nursing him, and with all his family around him he peacefully died.

Never give up hope for your family.

Acts 16:31 (NIV)
Believe on the Lord Jesus Christ and you will be saved, you and your household.

March 25th - *Study & Sermon notes*

Y1 – PS 24 / Y2 – PS 128

March 26th – *Gentle Challenge*
Y1 - ACTS 3 & 4 / Y2 – JOB 25 & 26

Matthew 18:20 (NKJV)
For where two or three are gathered in My name, I am there in the midst of them.

It's one thing to be in communion with God as an individual, but you step into another dimension of the Holy Spirit when you commune with fellow believers.

How often do you get together with other believers to talk about the things of God, study His word, and pray together?

The wife of a pastor is never without the need to be spiritually topped up. She is often at great risk of being diverted in her mind as she is typically consumed with 'doing,' but as we know, Jesus needs to come first. We love to give our time to many things, but time spent in the company of spiritual friends and other pastors' wives is essential.

I want to gently challenge you to start gathering with a few friends (every month or couple of months) to develop a new culture of lifting the name of Jesus together. In the comfort of your own home, you can sing, pray, and study scripture. You may not currently know any other local pastor's wives in your area, but I can assure you that they are there and in as much need for fellowship as you are. Get in tune, allow God to minister to you and through you, tap into the fruits and the gifts of the Holy Spirit, pray in tongues, give words, and heal the sick. Some of these are scary things to consider, but if God wills you to move in the gifts, it is important to sincerely contend for them.

In context, Jesus is confirming His presence when two or more agree together in dealing with a sinning brother, but he is giving us a wider truth as well. He says that when people come together with the aim of glorifying God, He will show up. He will be there listening, refilling, and responding to you. Arrange opportunities for you and your friends to tap into His presence and delight in the blessing it brings.

March 27th – *In Awe*
Y1 – ACT 5 & 6 / Y2 – JOB 27 & 28

Psalm 17:6 (NLT)
I am praying to you because I know you will answer, O God. Bend down and listen as I pray.

David's calm confidence during his crisis is encouraging. Though his problems were still present, he was confident that God would hear him when he called, prayed, and cried out to Him.

In the first few months of my salvation, I decided to establish a morning prayer routine and this is when it struck me, 'I am talking to God!' The Alpha and the Omega, creator of the universe, miracle worker, and life changer is listening to me! This revelation may seem comical and somewhat obvious, but can I ask you to ponder the question for a moment, *'How real is God to me?'*

After years of praying it can be so easy to take God's listening ears for granted.

Christianity is unique in that it is the only religion that encourages its believers to go straight into the throne room of God. We don't have to pray through a saint, a prophet, use repetitive mantras, or be in a sacred shrine on a special mat for our prayers to be recognised, but can speak boldly to our Saviour. We are blessed to access Jesus immediately with the assurance, if we are living righteously, that He digests, considers, and processes every word. It's a pretty powerful thing!

Heavenly Father, I am in awe of You. I thank You for wanting to have a relationship with me and for encouraging me to boldly approach You. I bring my prayer requests before You and believe that You will answer however you see fit, as it is Your will and not mine. Amen!

March 28th – *Great Epitaph*
Y1 – ACT 7 & 8 / Y2 – JOB 29 & 30

Luke 23:46 (NKJV)
And when Jesus had cried out with a loud voice, He said, 'Father, 'Into your hands I commit my spirit.' Having said this, He breathed His last.

The word Epitaph is defined as something by which a person, time, or event will be remembered.[1]

My husband once preached a sermon called 'Working towards a great epitaph' and it got me pondering. Think of this, Jesus is on the cross about to die and He said, 'It is finished (John 19:30)' and then His final words were, 'Father, Into your hands I commit my spirit (Luke 23:46).' He is at the end of His life and He has fulfilled the Father's plan.

I pondered this, and it really challenged me to live a fuller Christian life; that I might work towards and leave behind a legacy. Not just that I lived and was a Christian, but that I really made a difference to people, influencing their lives for good. Influence that resulted in salvation, causing them to live righteously, to be kind, generous, and wise. That it would be said of me that I was a good mother, a good wife, and obedient to God's will.

When it's our turn to go, *what are people going to say about our lives?* Will it be said, 'She really loved God and was obedient to the call of God; her life really counted?' It should be our desire to live the fullest life for Christ and work towards a great epitaph! *What can you do today to work towards that end?*

2 Timothy 4:7-8 (NIV)
I have fought the good fight, I have finished the race

March 29th – *Address Gossip*

Y1 – ACTS 9 & 10 / Y2 – JOB 31 & 32

Proverbs 26:27-28 (KJV)
Whoso diggeth a pit shall fall therein: and he that rolleth a stone, it will return upon him. A lying tongue hateth those that are afflicted by it; and a flattering mouth worketh ruin.

Gossip defined is 'unrestrained reports,' speaking carelessly without thinking, and as a result communicating information that is completely unnecessary and potentially harmful. Gossip can take many forms, but the common denominator is that it has no purpose and is never spoken from a heart of love. It is often an outward expression of our inner struggles and is unfortunately quite common amongst women (hopefully not Pastor's wives).

There is no excuse for speaking about others behind their backs! The Bible calls it a sin (Proverbs 16:28) and one that will keep you from heaven if unrepented (Revelations 21:8). Gossip, like any other sin, will bind you and hinder your access to God, His provisions and ultimately heaven. When identified in our life, it will take some mind consuming concentration to overcome, but believe me, gaining the ability (with the help of the Holy Spirit) to control your tongue will set you free.

Do you have a tendency to speak irresponsibly?

A conversation that 'digs' for information makes the recipient uncomfortable, so they mistrust you and back away. The harsh reality is that 'gossipers' are often surrounded by people (mostly other gossips) yet have few genuine friends. It takes courage, but for their sake this sin has to be challenged and carefully contended against, so it doesn't run its destructive course. Be the Christian without a hidden agenda that draws people to you because of your safe spirit and character that can lovingly maintain confidentiality.

Father, I repent. Forgive me for embracing and slipping into gossip. I recognise the need to restrain and retrain my tongue. Please set me free and help me overcome this subtle sin and rebuild credibility amongst friends and saints. Cause people to trust me again and see the change in me. Amen

March 30th – *Historical Women*
Y1 – ACTS 11 & 12 / Y2 – JOB 33 & 34

Elisabeth Elliott

Elisabeth was born in 1926 to missionary parents in Belgium but grew up in America. She felt if her heart was the Lord's then her body was also; so she committed to be a missionary and in 1944 enrolled at Wheaton College to study Greek.

Jim Elliot was also at the college, and though he fell in love with Elisabeth, he did not initially feel marriage was God's plan, but rather he felt called to be a missionary and potentially a martyr. They separately focused on God's call for their lives and after graduation Elisabeth went on a missionary expedition to Ecuador. Jim Elliot did also, working in a different region. In 1953, Jim felt that God was allowing him to marry Elisabeth, and so 5 years after initially meeting, they were married. The couple continued to serve in Ecuador, undeterred from their calling. In 1955, the same year they had their daughter Valerie, the missionaries initiated contact with the savage Aucas tribe.

A year later, Jim Elliot and four fellow missionary men were martyred by Auca spears. Elisabeth's heartbreak did not cause her to doubt what was started in faith and she continued to serve in Ecuador. That same year, she wrote the book Through the Gates of Splendour, inspiring untold numbers into the mission field. Elisabeth was still eager to bring salvation to the Aucas because the love of Jesus moved her to forgiveness. She continued working in the Quechua village but had two Auca women live with her allowing an opportunity for relationship building with the wider Auca tribe who were still unreached. In 1958, Elisabeth, her daughter Valerie, and Rachel Saint (a sister of one of the martyred missionaries) moved to live with the Auca tribe. The tribe saw and understood the forgiveness and grace that Elisabeth and Rachel extended to them and this was paramount in their conversion to Jesus. Elisabeth faced and overcame great trials, but through love and forgiveness was able to serve the people who killed her husband and lead many to receiving Christ.

March 31st - *Study & Sermon notes*

Y1 – PS 25 / Y2 – PS 129

Thank you for reading The Devotional Life of a Pastor's Wife.

Our prayer is for God to continually stir your heart and give you a fresh ability to minister with effectiveness and joy. But as this volume draws to a close, we are aware that the ministry can take its toll on the best of us. This can sometimes result in a crisis of faith that is difficult to talk about. If you find yourself in this position, we want to reassure you that you belong to a saviour who loves you today as much as the day you first received Him, and it is possible to start again. Here is a prayer of repentance for the woman whose heart has gone astray:

Father, I come before you today and acknowledge my sin. I repent of all unrighteousness and I am asking you to take lordship over my life and give me the strength to change. I believe that Jesus died and rose again on the third day and in faith I receive your forgiveness and salvation. I surrender my heart and future into your hands. Thank you, in Jesus name, Amen.

We encourage you to speak to your Pastor, husband or trusted spiritual friend about the decision you have made today. God's mercies are renewed every day and his love for you endures forever.

CONTACT US

(need a friend or want to share your story)

pwdevotional@outlook.com

WEBSITE

www.pwdevotion.co.uk

BOOK RECOMMENDATIONS

Lies women believe – Nancy Leigh Demoss

His needs her needs – Willard F Harley

Power through prayer – EM Bounds

Why standards – Jay Nembhard

Still taking the land – Wayman & Greg Mitchell

Disciplines of a Godly woman – Barbara Hughes

Zeal without burnout – Christopher Ash

Raising children/ Raising a strong-willed child/ Raising boy & raising girls – James Dobson

A surrendered wife – Laura Doyle

Deliverance to dominion *(How to gain control of your life)* – Joseph C Campbell & John W Gooding

How to win friends and influence people – Dale Carnegie

Chasing the dragon- Jackie Pullinger

Run baby run- Nicky Cruz

The cross and the switchblade- David Wilkerson

Gay girl, good God – Jackie Hill Perry

Armed and dangerous – John Ramirez

More than a carpenter – Josh McDowell

The case for Christ- Lee Strobel

Let me be a woman – Elisabeth Elliott

The money secret -Rob Parsons

Deadly emotions – Don Colbert

APPENDIX

January 9th – Famous Four
1- Merriam Webster, 2020, *Abandon Definition,* accessed 27/08/2020
<https://www.merriam-webster.com/dictionary/abandon#h1>

January 22nd – Great Epitaph
1- Oxford Dictionary, Lexico, 2020, accessed 11/09/2020
https://www.lexico.com/definition/epitaph

January 29th – Discerning Spirit
1- Cambridge Dictionary, 2020, accessed
06/2020https://dictionary.cambridge.org/dictionary/english/discern
2- Strong's dictionary, 2004-2020, accessed 06/2020
https://biblehub.com/str/greek/2529.htm

Wikipedia, 2020, accessed
06/2020https://en.wikipedia.org/wiki/Discernmen

January 31st – Seeking Spirituality
1- Peck. A pg1

https://www.spirituality-for-life.org/pdf-
files/WhatIsChristianSpirituality.pdf#:~:text=Christian%20spirituality%20is%2
0the%20conscious%20human%20response%20to,people.6%20He%20is%20im
manent%20in%20all%20relationships.7%20By

February 5th – Jehovah God
1- Names of God by Nathan Stone, 2010 edition, page 33
2- Names of God by Nathan Stone, 2010 edition, page 34
3- Strong's Dictionary, King James Bible Dictionary, 2020
http://kingjamesbibledictionary.com/StrongsNo/H3068/GOD/0
4- Names of God by Nathan Stone, 2010 edition, page 39-40

February 14th – Prayer Covering
1- BibleRef, 2002-2020, accessed on 08/09/20 https://www.bibleref.com/1-
Peter/3/1-Peter-3-7.html

February 21st – Shimmering Saint
1- oxford dictionary 28.08.20 definition of sanctified

February 22nd – Arising mother
1- Deep Spirituality, 2019, *7 Examples of Trusting God in Difficult Times to
Inspire You, accessed 21/07/2020* <https://deepspirituality.net/trusting-god-
in-difficult-times/>

February 23rd – Historical Women
1- 50 women every Christian should know: pg 125- 131 M.Derusha 2014
edition

March 1st – Missionaries Wife
1- Adam Clarke's Commentary, StudyLight, 2001-2020, accessed on 16/09/2020
https://www.studylight.org/commentaries/acc/matthew-19.html

March 5th – Mighty El-Shaddai
1- E Teacher Biblical, 2020, Names of God - El-Shaddai, accessed 05/08/2020, <http://eteacherbiblical.com/articles/el-shaddai>

2- Bible Study Tools, 2020, *Genesis 17,* accessed 05/08/2020, <http://www.biblestudytools.com/commentaries/scofield-reference-notes/genesis/genesis-17.html>

March 6th – Be Acknowledged
1- Barnes, A. (1851) Notes on the New Testament Explanatory and Practical. Blackie

March 8th – Program Princess
1- Alfred Edersheim and Dr. Doug Bookman, 2010, *Who was Nicodemus in the Bible and Was He Saved? Christianity.com,* accessed 28/08/2020, <https://www.christianity.com/jesus/life-of-jesus/disciples/was-nicodemus-a-follower-of-christ.html>

March 16th – Proverbs 31:12-16
1- Enduring Word, 2020, accessed 07/2020
https://enduringword.com/bible-commentary/proverbs-31/

March 22nd – Perfected Faith
1- Enduringword, 2020 accessed 29/08/2020
https://enduringword.com/bible-commentary/james-2/
2- Matthew Henry's commentary, Biblehub, 2004-2020, accessed 29/08/2020
https://biblehub.com/commentaries/james/2-22.htm

March 23rd – Picture Perfect
1- Chara Donahue, 2020, *How Jesus Practiced Hospitality (Without a Home) and Generosity (Without a Salary),* iBelieve, accessed 28/08/2020, <https://www.ibelieve.com/food-home/how-jesus-practiced-hospitality-without-a-home-and-generosity-without-a-salary.html>
2- Jon Bloom, 2017, *Lay Aside the Weight of Perfection,* Desiring God, accessed 28/08/2020, <https://www.desiringgod.org/articles/lay-aside-the-weight-of-perfection

COLOSSIANS 2:6-7 (NKJV)

As you therefore have received Christ Jesus the Lord, so walk in Him, rooted and built up in Him and established in the faith, as you have been taught, abounding in it with thanksgiving.

Printed in Great Britain
by Amazon

54975283R00075